PRAISE FOR

GOD ENCOUNTERS

Jesus said that to know God *is* eternal life (see John 17:3). Through this study of His Word, Elmer L. Towns helps us to encounter and know our heavenly Father more intimately. Nothing could be more important.

BILL BRIGHT
FOUNDER AND PRESIDENT
CAMPUS CRUSADE FOR CHRIST INTERNATIONAL
ORLANDO, FLORIDA

I have known Elmer Towns for 30 years, and I know of no one more qualified to write a book on encountering God. He taught this subject here at Thomas Road Baptist Church, and the people felt closer to God as a result of this teaching, which was perhaps his most effective ever. *God Encounters* will help you to meet our Lord, and when you do, you will know and experience Him.

JERRY FALWELL
PASTOR, THOMAS ROAD BAPTIST CHURCH
LYNCHBURG, VIRGINIA

What an encouragement to know that God breaks into our lives at unexpected times! Through biblical and contemporary stories, Elmer Towns admonishes us to detect the hand of God in our lives today. I was uplifted and instructed, and you will be, too.

ERWIN W. LUTZER

SENIOR PASTOR, MOODY CHURCH
CHICAGO, ILLINOIS

Elmer Towns has given us an insightful and encouraging word on an incredibly important subject. *God Encounters* will be a source of strength for every Christian who reads it. I am glad to recommend this book.

ADRIAN ROGERS

PASTOR, BELLEVUE BAPTIST CHURCH
CORDOVA, TENNESSEE

Elmer Towns has done the Body of Christ a great service by giving us *God Encounters*. The easy-reading format is very inviting. Dr. Towns offers hope that everyone of us can and should experience a personal encounter with God. I pray this book will help you make fresh contact with the living God.

STEVE WINGFIELD

EVANGELIST AND PRESIDENT, WINGFIELD MINISTRIES
HARRISONBURG, VIRGINIA

GOD
ENCOUNTERS

TO TOUCH GOD
AND BE TOUCHED BY HIM

ELMER L. TOWNS

Regal

A Division of Gospel Light
Ventura, California, U.S.A.

Published by Regal Books
A Division of Gospel Light
Ventura, California, U.S.A.
Printed in U.S.A.

Cover Design by Kevin Keller
Interior Design by Robert Williams
Edited by Kathi Mills and Wil Simon

LIBRARY OF CONGRESS CATALOGING-IN-PUBLICATION DATA
Towns, Elmer L.
    God encounters / Elmer L. Towns
    p. cm.
    Includes bibliographical references.
    ISBN 0-8307-2336-6 (trade paper)
    1. Christian life. 2. Presence of God. 3. Bible—Biography. I. Title.

BV4509.5 .T69 2000   99-087088
231.7—dc21

1 2 3 4 5 6 7 8 9 10 11 12 13 14 15 / 07 06 05 04 03 02 01 00

Rights for publishing this book in other languages are contracted by Gospel Literature
International (GLINT). GLINT also provides technical help for the adaptation, translation
and publishing of Bible study resources and books in scores of languages world-
wide. For further information, write to GLINT at P.O. Box 4060, Ontario, CA 91761-1003,
U.S.A. You may also send e-mail to Glintint@aol.com, or visit the GLINT website at
www.glint.org.

CONTENTS

Foreword 9
Hungry for God—*Tommy Tenney*

Introduction 11
Encountering God to Transform Your Life

Snapshot 1 23
Having a King for a Friend—*Jack Hayford*

Chapter 1 29
Abraham: Becoming a Friend with God
An encounter based on friendship. On a hot day, God visited Abraham's tent to fellowship with him. Abraham was so intimate with God that even God wouldn't keep a secret from him.

Snapshot 2 41
Face-to-Face Five Times—*John Maxwell*

Chapter 2 47
Jacob: Seeing God Face-to-Face
An encounter out of fear. Jacob wrestled all night with God and wouldn't let Him go. Because of Jacob's tenacity, God blessed him and changed his name to Israel, i.e., a Prince with God.

Snapshot 3 61
The Courage from God—*Billy Graham*

Chapter 3 63
Moses: The Servant of God
An encounter out of frustration. God said Moses was the meekest man on the face of the earth, yet Moses boldly asked to see God's glory. When he saw the backside of God, his face shone for 40 days.

Snapshot 4 . . . .**77**
Overcoming Fear—*John Wesley*

Chapter 4 . . . .**81**
Gideon: A Reluctant Leader

An encounter out of weak self-image. Gideon was at the bottom of the social ladder and filled with self-doubt when he encountered God. Because of that experience, Gideon was able to drive the enemy out of his homeland.

Snapshot 5 . . . .**93**
A New Morning—*Joe Focht*

Chapter 5 . . . .**95**
Elijah: Hearing God's Small Voice

An encounter out of discouragement. Elijah ran into the desert because Queen Jezebel threatened to kill him. He encountered God, not in a mighty force to destroy the evil rule of Jezebel, but in a still, small voice to send Elijah back into service.

Snapshot 6 . . . .**107**
Awakened Zeal—*Oswald Chambers*

Chapter 6 . . . .**111**
Isaiah: Prophet for God

An encounter when dreams are destroyed. Isaiah put his dreams in a king who died, then he saw the Lord. That encounter changed him forever, and he became God's prophet who wrote one of the most beautiful books in the Bible.

Snapshot 7 . . . . **123**
Nose-to-the-Ground Humility—*Adrian Rogers*

Chapter 7 . . . . **127**
Jeremiah: Weeping for God
*An encounter to be built up for a call to service. God set Jeremiah apart
for ministry from His mother's womb. God later encountered 21-year-
old Elijah to call him to a ministry of rejection and persecution.*

Snapshot 8 . . . . **139**
A Persistent Vision for the World—
Richard C. Halverson

Chapter 8 . . . . **143**
Ezekiel: Seeing Visions for God
*An encounter for a new calling. Ezekiel was a priest who was trained
for Temple service, but he encountered God in a vision in which he
saw extraordinary sights. Out of that encounter, he became a prophet
who communicated a vision of Israel's future Temple.*

Snapshot 9 . . . . **155**
The Sweet Touch of God for Healing—
V. Raymond Edman

Chapter 9 . . . . **159**
The Woman with the Issue of Blood
*An encounter for healing. A woman thought a slight touch of the hem
of Jesus' coat would heal her, but she was encountered by Jesus to
learn that it was her faith that made her whole.*

Snapshot 10 173
Seeing Christ Among the Children—*Amy Carmichael*

Chapter 10 177
Mary Magdalene: Taught by Christ
An encounter to learn spiritual relationship. Mary came to the garden to care for a corpse. When she saw Jesus, she hung on to His physical feet to renew the love she had for Him before the cross. In an encounter with Christ, she learned that she would relate to Him "in the Spirit" in the future.

Snapshot 11 187
The Power to Preach—*Dwight Lyman Moody*

Chapter 11 189
Peter: A Backslider Restored to Service
An encounter to be restored to service. Peter denied the Lord through boasting and pride. After breakfast on a beach, Jesus restored him to service and he became a bold preacher on the day of Pentecost.

Snapshot 12 201
A Dynamic Change—*Charles Grandison Finney*

Chapter 12 203
Saul: Becoming a Follower of Christ
An encounter to change the mind. Paul hated Christians, yet encountered Christ on the road to Damascus where his life was transformed. Paul received his commission from this experience.

Epilogue 219
Your Blueprint for an Encounter with God

Finis 227

HUNGRY FOR GOD

The third Sunday of October 1996 I had a God encounter. I will never be the same. Even my friends still remark, "What happened to you?" I used to be a bit reluctant to say I had encountered God, but Isaiah said it: "I saw the Lord" (Isa. 6:1). If he could say it, so can I.

My heart thumped with trepidation and excitement when Elmer Towns asked me to do the foreword for his book *God Encounters.* Thrilled that he would honor me by asking, and excited to read what Elmer had written, I was also afraid the general public wouldn't understand this subject and might trample the topic with banalities, trashing sacred memories of mine and others who have had God encounters. My fears were washed away by the brilliant writing and the theological soundness of the manuscript. *Dr. Towns, you did good!* It's impossible to read this book and not be convinced and challenged to pursue an encounter of your own.

If you've ever met Him, you can instantly tell the difference between somebody who's just seen a picture or someone who actually *met* Him! They smell like smoke and fire, incense and blood! There's a special look in their eyes, a wavering crack in their voice when they begin to talk about "the encounter." And they usually can remember the exact date it happened. Elmer Towns displays all those characteristics in this book. He had a God encounter!

Drawing from a rich religious heritage and a lineage of long-lasting friendships with major figures in contemporary Christianity, Elmer weaves the past with the present, biblical encounters with modern rendezvous. The result is a very practical road map for others to use to arrive at a divine destination. Following this road map will get you in God's vicinity; you'll have to finish the search on your own, but you'll be closer for having read this book.

Elmer Towns tells us how *anywhere* can become *somewhere*, how *anyplace* can become *someplace*, how *anytime* can become *sometime*, and how *anybody* can become *somebody* by encountering God for spiritual breakthrough!

He is such a storytelling wordsmith that he makes the mystical no longer a mystery. He breathes fresh life into biblical encounters, making them seem recent. In this book, his gift of teaching is so apparent that anyone can follow the crumbs of knowledge to the place of His presence.

Explaining the difference between getting saved and having a power encounter with the living God, creates hunger in me. In fact there's nothing like reading from the menu to make you ravenous! Elmer Towns has laid out the menu of His Majesty in rare form.

I'm hungry right now.

Tommy Tenney
Author of *The GodChasers* . . . still chasing

ENCOUNTERING GOD TO TRANSFORM YOUR LIFE

The idea of this book came to me on the 39th day of a 40-day fast. In this fast, I was asking God to show me what to write in a book to bless the lives of His Church. I met an editor who asked what was the greatest answer to prayer during my fast. I had something better; I answered, "I've learned to know God . . . I've met God."

"Why don't you write how people can encounter God?" he suggested.

I wrote this book and then sent the manuscript to the editor. He read it and then suggested the book needed one additional item. "Readers will want to know about your own encounters with God," he told me. "Including that will give credibility to the book."

Encountering God
for Salvation

When I was in the first grade, a door-to-door salesman invited me to Sunday School. He picked me up in his Jewell Tea Coffee truck, and after that I never missed for the next 14 years. I studied the Bible and each week memorized the "Golden Scripture" text, as well as the children's catechism. I didn't have the experience of alcohol, drugs or crime before my conversion. I was a typical southern boy who grew up doing the typical things that American boys do.

All the young people in our youth group joined the church on Easter Sunday, 1944. We were asked if we believed in the great fundamental doctrines of the faith.

"I believe," was my response. I accepted the death of Jesus as fact, just as I accepted all the truth taught me in public school. I joined the Presbyterian church, took communion and did all the things that Presbyterians are supposed to do. The only problem was that I did not know Jesus Christ as my personal Savior. Then, in July 1950, I attended a revival meeting in a small Presbyterian church in Bonnabella, Georgia. The atmospheric presence of God was felt in that revival during the singing and preaching, but especially when the invitation was given. As people experienced God's presence, they went to the church altar where they prayed to receive Christ.

Revival swept through the community. The rural mailman attended the service, went forward to kneel at the altar and prayed to receive Christ. As the meeting came to an end, he stood before the congregation to say that he knew most everyone present by name. He announced to that congregation, "I joined a Baptist church, sang in the choir, was a deacon and the Sunday

School superintendent; but tonight I was born again."

The mailman explained that there were 23 churches on his route, and he didn't feel anything special from them as he delivered mail each day—except from this church. He confessed, "About a half a block away, I could feel something special about this place." He claimed it was the presence of God. "As I drove away from this church, I could feel it going away." The mailman was describing what some call the atmospheric presence of God. There are times in worship or evangelistic services when people can actually feel God's presence.

On July 25, during the second week of the crusade, no one went forward. It was the first evening that no one prayed to receive Christ. There was genuine disappointment among the congregation because they thought God hadn't worked in hearts that evening. The pastor came down in front of the communion table to announce, "Somebody here should have come forward this evening." He paused to let his words sink in. He seemed to be speaking directly to me. "You were embarrassed to come forward, even though you know God was telling you to become a Christian."

I was dumbfounded because he had described my feelings. During the invitational hymn, I felt God telling me to go forward to get saved. But I struggled with the Lord, telling him I was already a Christian; I had joined the church; I had believed that Jesus died for me. I didn't realize that a person could have a historical belief about Jesus without possessing Him as Savior. The pastor then told us, "If you were supposed to come forward tonight and were afraid," he paused to tell us what to do, "I want you to go home, kneel by your bed, look into heaven, tell Jesus you have never done it before, then ask Him into your heart."

Standing toward the back of the auditorium, I determined to do what he said when I got home; but when I got home, I changed my mind. I knelt to pray the Lord's Prayer and then got in bed. But I couldn't go to sleep because I felt guilty for not doing what I needed to do. I got out of bed to pray:

Now I lay me down to sleep,
I pray the Lord my soul to keep.
If I should die before I wake,
I pray the Lord, my soul to take.

It was the prayer I had prayed as a child on a number of occasions, the prayer taught to me by my mother. I got back into bed but couldn't go to sleep. God was talking to me, telling me to do what the minister asked. On two or three more occasions that night I got out of bed, each time to pray either the Lord's Prayer or "Now I lay me down . . ."

In my head I kept saying I was a Christian because I had joined the church and I had historical faith in Jesus Christ. Finally, I knelt by my bed, looked up into heaven and willingly prayed as the pastor had told me to do. I prayed sincerely, "Lord, I've never done it before . . ."

When I honestly came to the conviction that I was not saved—and told God I was not saved—I felt the horror of hell. It was as though I looked over a wall into hell and felt its terror. For just a few seconds I felt fear unlike anything I had felt before. Then quickly I prayed, "Lord Jesus, come into my heart and save me." Electricity went through me. I knew that I had put my faith in Jesus Christ, and I knew I was going to heaven. Jesus was real to me—not physically in my bedroom, but He was alive in my heart. I felt peace like I had never felt before—security. I also felt excitement. I whispered a shout, "Amen . . . Hallelujah . . . Praise the Lord!" I jumped to my feet and lifted one hand to heaven in whispered praise. Because my father was drunk in the next bed, I couldn't talk out loud, so I whispered my shouts to God: "I am saved!"

I could feel the presence of Jesus, and I talked to Him. I sang a hymn silently:

Amazing grace, how sweet the sound,
That saved a wretch like me.
I once was lost, but now I'm found;
Was blind but now I see.

This manuscript tells the stories of people in the Bible who encountered God; some of the encounters resulted in their conversion. Saul was an enemy of God until he met Jesus Christ on a road to Damascus. Gideon was probably like me, a person who knew religious language and religious practices, but was converted when he encountered God. But there were other occasions in my life where I encountered God and changed my plans.

ENCOUNTERING GOD FOR DIRECTION

I had been teaching in a Bible college for three years when I woke up violently in the middle of a black night. Something was wrong. I began to sweat all over.

"Lord, what is it?"

The Lord was in the room, not physically, nor did I see a vision, nor did I hear an audible voice; but I knew that the Lord was standing by my bed to warn me of something.

I immediately thought of a burglar and that gave me an additional fear. Then I thought perhaps there was a fire, or someone I knew was in danger or dying. I prayed several times, "Lord, what are you trying to tell me?"

Then the Lord spoke to my heart, telling me not to take the new job I had just accepted. A few days earlier, I had resigned my job teaching in a Bible college to join the National Sunday School Association to travel to different denominations and Sunday School conventions to challenge people with a vision of Sunday School. It was a perfect job: travel, influence, ministry in many churches and national recognition. But as I lay in bed, I knew God was telling me, "Don't take the Sunday School job."

I wrestled with the Lord in my bed because I knew the Sunday School job had great potential. It would be exciting, I would be well known, and I would influence a lot more people than teaching at Midwest Bible College, St. Louis, which had only 150 students at that time.

"Don't take the job," God kept saying.

As I wrestled with God, I reviewed my long-range priorities. I asked myself what those priorities were. I also asked what were my strongest gifts and how I could make the greatest contribution with my life. I confessed to the Lord that I was ego driven. Ever since I was a freshman in Bible college, I wanted to be a Bible-college president. I had rationalized that the fame I would get from the new position of traveling for Sunday School would open up a door into a Bible college somewhere, sometime. But every time I talked to God, I got the same message: "Don't take the Sunday School job."

After a couple of hours of praying, I surrendered before the Lord. I told Him that fame was not important. I surrendered my reputation and even said, "God, if I never become a Bible-college president, Thy will be done!"

When I finally surrendered my will to God, I thought I heard God say, "Don't take the Sunday School job . . . but within a year I will give you a college presidency."

By faith I accepted God's will for my life, and I signed a contract at Midwest Bible College for the coming year. I resigned the new position with the National Sunday School Association.

ENCOUNTER WITH GOD FOR A CALL TO MINISTRY

Six months later I had an encounter with God that changed my direction of ministry. Just as Jeremiah had his ministry changed, as well as Isaiah and Ezekiel, I heard from God in an unusual way. On a snowy winter day, I had taken a longer way home from the college, driving past my church, Hope Congregational. I saw tracks in the snow up the front drive and, as I drove past, I looked back to see the pastor's car in his usual parking spot. I turned around to go back just to chat. After a few minutes of talking, I told Pastor Robert Macmillan, "I want to be a Bible-college president someday."

Macmillan was very close to the ministry of Midwest Bible College and had served on several committees at the college. He immediately reinforced my lifelong goal when he said, "That's wonderful. A man like you has the drive and ability to be a Bible-college president. I think you'll make a wonderful college president."

The phone rang. Dr. Stuart Boehmer, a pastor in Toronto, Canada, was on the line. Boehmer was a close friend with Robert Macmillan. After they greeted one another with pleasantries, Boehmer asked Macmillan, "Do you know where we can find a young man to be president of Winnipeg Bible College?"

"Your man is sitting right here," Macmillan said into the phone.

In the predetermined will of God, there is no such thing as a coincidence; all things work together for the purpose of God.

The chairman of Winnipeg Bible College, Manitoba, had driven 1,200 miles to Toronto looking for a Bible-college president. While I was talking about being a college president, the Bible-college chairman, Frank Frogley, was asking Stuart Boehmer to help find a college president. So, Stuart Boehmer said to Macmillan, "I have a man here in my office who is looking for a president. Let's put them on the phone together and see if it's a match."

For approximately 30 minutes, Frank Frogley and I discussed Winnipeg Bible College. We discussed strategy, purpose, theology . . . but most of all we discussed the will of God. While we were talking on the phone, I could hear the voice of God whispering in my other ear, "See . . . I told you that if you wouldn't take the Sunday School job, I'd have a college presidency for you within a year."

Before the conversation was over, I knew God would give the presidency to me. Then, as a seal from God, Frank Frogley concluded the conversation. "You're my man. I am getting in my car tomorrow morning to drive to St. Louis to interview you."

The board at Winnipeg Bible College had rejected a number of candidates, but when Frank Frogley recommended me, I got the position.

My experience of encountering God is probably not an example that may happen to you. We are all different: different personalities, different callings, different backgrounds, different purposes in life. God meets us differently, and God leads us differently. There's not a perfect way to experience God, so be careful that you don't try to emulate my encounter, nor should you try to do the exact things of others who have encountered God.

I've included 12 stories in this book of people in the Bible who encountered God. You can rely on their truthfulness because the stories are from the Bible. Also, you will learn how to encounter God because the stories are from God.

You can know God like Abraham, who encountered God and was called the friend of God, i.e., *el Kahil*. The encounter changed Abraham's life; it was so awesome . . . life changing . . . revolutionary. You can learn from his encounter with God and walk with God.

EXTRAORDINARY EXPERIENCES— A FEW ENCOUNTER GOD; MOST WILL NOT. WILL YOU?

Learn how Moses' face shone for 40 days after he encountered God. Learn how Jacob limped for the rest of his life after encountering God. Something died when Paul met Jesus Christ on the road to Damascus. After his encounter with Christ, Paul faced death so many times: beatings, shipwrecks, stoning, robbery. He lived as though he didn't fear death because the old Paul had died when he encountered Christ. A new Paul unselfishly served the Lord after that experience. Learn how you can fearlessly stare death in the face like Paul. Would you like to meet Christ in a cool morning garden like Mary Magdalene? Look for biblical principles at the end of each chapter to guide your experience with God.

What does it mean to encounter God? The best way to describe an encounter with God is to tell you what it is not. An encounter is not just praying to God. An encounter may happen when you pray, but it's infinitely more; and it happens usually only once—or a few times—in a lifetime.

An encounter is not just meeting with God for your daily quiet time, although you will meet with God many times in your life. An encounter is life changing, because the presence of God will become so extraordinarily real. The encounter will include some momentous circumstances that will not happen again.

An encounter is not a place where you worship God, such as a chapel, or at the altar during a camp meeting. An encounter is not just His anointing on your service. Nor is an encounter an insightful result of Bible study. However, an encounter will happen at some specific location, you will be anointed because of it, and you will receive great insights from it.

Some, such as Isaiah, Jeremiah or Ezekiel, encounter God at the beginning of a life of profitable service. Others, such as John on the Isle of Patmos, encounter God at the end of a life faithfully serving God.

Some will refuse to read this book because they wrongly think God only encounters the "good guys." They will wrongly think they can't experience God because they don't live close to God. But look closely at the incidents in this book. You may encounter God no matter how unspiritual you may think you are. Jacob was still trying one more "trick" to get out of trouble when he encountered God. Elijah was discouraged; he was running from his enemies when God turned him around. Peter had boasted about his boldness, then denied Christ three times. After being utterly disgraced, Peter encountered Christ. And don't forget about the Christian-bashing Paul who encountered Christ on the Damascus road. What does this mean?

You can encounter God!

All the encounters in this book were at different places and at different times and involved different motivations. Study each one carefully to find similarities between them. In each experience, God and a person meet. Don't try to duplicate their experiences; rather, study carefully the encounters to find principles that will help you encounter God for your personal needs.

If you read these stories and think you cannot encounter God in this life, read the epilogue. The principles of encountering God are found there, as well as a prescription for you to encounter God. Anyone may encounter God—even you.

Along with reading these stories, go study the Scriptures where these encounters took place. Look up the geographical places in a Bible dictionary. Study the personalities to know their strengths, weaknesses and dreams. It may be that in your Bible study you will meet God face-to-face.

These encounters are written in modern dialogue to help you feel the emotions of each experience. While not every conversation and activity are included in Bible narrative, they come out of the historical background of each story. The Bible is interpreted according to evangelical scholars' understanding of each event.

This book was written after my 40-day fast was over, but I learned many of its lessons long before I fasted. I've been studying the Bible diligently since I was converted in 1950. This book is the result of a lifelong pilgrimage to understand what it means to encounter God.

May God bless this book and use what is useful. May God forgive the limitations of this book, for they are mine alone. May God bless you as you read, and may you know God, and make Him known.

Written from my home in the Blue Ridge Mountains of Virginia,

Elmer Towns
Summer 1998

HAVING A KING
FOR A FRIEND*

DR. JACK HAYFORD
PASTOR, THE CHURCH ON THE WAY
VAN NUYS, CALIFORNIA

We stood in silent awe, sensing God's presence as shafts of sunlight arrowed through the gracefully arched windows high in the vaulted towers of the vacant abbey. The British countryside was welcoming another summer's morn as we ambled through the partially restored ruins of this ancient house of worship.

For two weeks, my wife, Anna, and I had been probing the corners of Scotland, Wales and England in our tiny rental car, setting our own pace as we drove from place to place. We chose a leisurely pace, visiting castles and cottages at our whim. On a side trip we made into Oxfordshire, an illusive sense of the grand, the regal and the noble came by surprise and included a lesson I hadn't expected and resulted in a song I hadn't sought.

Blenheim Palace is the massive estate built at Queen Anne's orders in the early eighteenth century. She presented it to John Churchill, the first duke of Marlborough, in honor of his leadership in the military victories against Spain. Two centuries later, Winston Churchill would be born and raised here, frequently retiring to this site for rest from the rigors of leadership during World War II. It was at Blenheim that many of his stirring speeches were written, speeches that successfully inspired the English people to sustain their efforts at staving off Hitler's Luftwaffe.

After we passed outside and surveyed the sprawling grounds so meticulously groomed and magnificently flowered, the undefined feeling now surfaced and blossomed into a clear, complete thought. While overlooking the palace and grounds from the southwest and contemplating Churchill's former presence on the paths and fields, I mused aloud: "Being raised in such an environment would certainly make it far more credible for a person to conceive of himself as a person of destiny."

Even as I stood there, millions of common folk of ordinary means were enthused and excited about celebrating one woman's (Queen Elizabeth's) royal ascent a quarter of a century earlier. It seemed inescapably linked in some mystical way to the fact that each one perceived himself linked with and personally represented by the one who wears the crown and bears the scepter, a national dignity that flows to the general citizenry from the regal office of a single individual who reigns over them, exercising authority as an ennobled friend rather than as a feudal overlord.

Then a second thought exploded: This is the essence of the relationship Jesus wants us to have with His church! He wants the fullness of His power, the richness of His nature, the authority of His office and the wealth of His resources to ennoble our identity and determine our destiny!

Notwithstanding the deep emotion filling my soul, a holy calm and genuine joy possessed me. Standing there, my gaze sweeping the scene once again—verdant, lush fields, fragrance of roses everywhere, magnificence in architecture with the stateliness of historic bearing—I gently squeezed Anna's hand.

"Honey, I can hardly describe to you all the things which this setting evokes in me. There is something of a majesty in all this, and I believe it has a great deal to do with why people who lived here have been of such consequence in the shaping of history. I don't mean that buildings and beauty can beget greatness, but I do feel that some people fail to perceive their possibilities because of their dismal surroundings."

As we continued our walk, I spoke further of my concerns with which she agreed. She felt, as I did, a pastoral longing for people to understand the fullness of Jesus, to perceive His high destiny for each of them—to see that our self-realization only comes through a real-realization of Him! How completely and unselfishly He invites us to partnership with Him in His Kingdom. How much of His Kingdom authority He wants to transmit to and through us as a flow of His life, love and healing to a hopeless and hurting world.

Now something expanding and deepening that understanding was welling up within me.

Majesty.

The word was crisp in my mind.

Majesty, I thought. It's the quality of Christ's royalty and

Kingdom glory that not only displays His excellence but which also lifts us by His sheer grace and power, allowing us to identify with and share in His wonder.

Majesty.

As Queen Elizabeth's throne somehow dignifies every Englishman and makes multitudes of others partakers in a commonwealth of royal heritage, our ascended Savior sits enthroned and offers His regal resources to each of us.

Majesty.

As a nation rose against the personification of evil in the Nazi scourge, ignited to action by a leader who perceived himself a person of destiny, created by a childhood identification with the majestic, so may the Church arise.

The crowds were increasing at Blenheim, and the marvel of the moment seemed no less real for becoming less intimate. "Let's go, honey," I said, and we started for the car. My soul was still resonating to the sound of a distant chord struck in heaven.

As Anna and I drove along the narrow highway, the road undulating from one breathtaking view to another, I said to her, "Take the notebook and write down some words, will you, babe?"

I began to dictate the key, the musical notes, the time value of each and the lyrics (and she still insists that *she* wrote the song!):

Majesty, worship His Majesty!
Unto Jesus be all glory, honor and praise.
Majesty, Kingdom authority,
Flows from His Throne, unto His own,
His anthem raise.

So exalt, lift up on high the name of Jesus.
Magnify, come glorify, Christ Jesus the King.

Majesty, worship His Majesty.
Jesus who died, now glorified,
King of all kings.

* Jack Hayford, Introduction to *Worship His Majesty* (Ventura, CA: Regal Books, 2000).

CHAPTER 1

ABRAHAM:
BECOMING A FRIEND WITH GOD

ENCOUNTER: BASED ON FRIENDSHIP
PLACE: AT A TENT IN THE HILLS OF JUDEA
SCRIPTURE: GENESIS 18

The frail 99-year-old man sat cross-legged at the entrance to his great Bedouin tent, the entry flap propped up as shade to protect him from the blistering sun. His eyes were closed to shut out its blinding reflection. It was hot—120°—too hot even for a slight breeze. A fly buzzed around his face, but the heat made it too uncomfortable to swat it away.

Abraham's camp was set on top of a hill that gave him a view in every direction. He could even see down into the Jordan River valley and the Dead Sea some 20 miles away. The highway through the valley ran along the sea into the towns of Sodom and Gomorrah. From his camp, Abraham could see the whole valley.

Suddenly, one of Abraham's two dozen servants pointed down the trail. "Look, Master. Three travelers are coming this way."

"Who are they?" old Abraham asked as he rose, shielding his eyes from the sun with his hands. "No travelers use this mountain trail."

The main highway between Jericho and Sodom, where the caravans traveled, stretched along the Dead Sea in the flat valley. Abraham lived in the top of the hills, where travel was difficult. Visitors to his camp were rare.

"Come," Abraham commanded his servant, walking briskly down the path to greet the strangers. The camp stirred with excitement. Visitors in the camp meant a special banquet that night, as well as a chance to catch up on the news.

"Greetings!" Abraham's voice cracked as he attempted to yell out to the three visitors. They returned his greetings, acknowledging him as he bowed in oriental fashion.

"If I have found grace in your sight," said Abraham with a smile, "if you will look on me as your host, I will give you water to drink . . . wash your feet . . . a morsel of bread"—Abraham interrupted his speech, turning to point to a nearby oak tree. "Come rest a while. Cool off; let me prepare an evening meal." Waiting for a response, Abraham offered, "Eat with us; then you can continue traveling."

The leader of the three men accepted his hospitality. "We will eat with you."

Abraham made sure his guests found a comfortable place under the spreading oak tree, then he walked briskly toward his tent, barking orders as he walked through the tent flaps.

Abraham's camp sprang to life. No one paid attention to the heat any longer. Consumed with their tasks, comfort took a backseat to their passion. Abraham allowed the visitors to recline in the shade, not disturbing their rest. As the sun began to set, a refreshing breeze stirred in the valley. Crickets began to chirp as Abraham called, "Our food is ready."

The meal was superb; the warm roasted beef was tender, butter melted on the biscuits. The emerging stars beginning to twinkle in the early evening were the canopy for this banquet hall.

The leader of the three strangers offered appreciation to Abraham for the meal. Shortly after, Abraham and his guests retired to sit around the fire at the door to Abraham's tent.

"Tell us of the world . . ." Abraham began. But the travelers hadn't come to share social news; they had another purpose.

"Where is Sarah, your wife?"

Abraham nodded toward the tent, knowing Sarah would be listening at the door.

The leader of the group spoke. "I will return to your wife the ability to have children." The shock effect on Abraham was indescribable as the leader continued speaking. "Sarah will conceive and deliver a son."

Abraham's emotions went wild. The childless man had always wanted a son. Now this visitor had declared it would happen. Abraham had obeyed God in Chaldea when God commanded him to leave his homeland and come to this land. Abraham believed God when the Lord told him that he would have more children than grains of sand on the beaches. But that was 24 years ago, Sarah had not conceived, and they were past the age for childbearing.

Abraham remembered that 14 years ago he took an Egyptian maid—Hagar—and together they had a son. But that boy was not the spiritual heir God had promised. Now Abraham was being told that 89-year-old Sarah would get pregnant and have a son.

"How can this happen?" Abraham asked, staring at the red coals becoming brighter as the evening grew darker.

After a moment the leader spoke. "I will return her youth. Is anything too hard for the Lord?"

With that question, Abraham turned his attention to the speaker. The frail old man had been so concerned about himself and his son that he forgot about the One who was speaking to him. Abraham knew that only God could do miracles, only God could turn back the inevitable creeping age in all people. He realized he was entertaining deity in his camp. God had sent His presence in a human form to dine at his table. Abraham believed, but didn't understand.

The two new friends conversed intimately. Few get an opportunity to talk this way with God. But few have such deep faith that God is able to commune with them, for a conversation with God is two-sided.

As Abraham talked with God, he forgot that Sarah was listening in the tent. She heard what the stranger said about her conceiving in her old age. She heard the spokesman tell her husband that she was going to have a son, but she didn't believe it. She had heard many wild tales by men around the campfire. She knew that men boasted . . . and bragged. She didn't take the prediction seriously.

"Ha!" Sarah laughed.

Sarah knew God had promised her husband a son, but she had been barren since her wedding day. Sarah knew that God had said Abraham's children would be more than the sand on the beaches, but God never promised her a son. She knew Abraham had faith in God to do anything, but she knew old women didn't have babies. She merely laughed in unbelief.

But God heard Sarah laugh because God knows everything. Though Sarah didn't laugh loudly enough to be heard outside the tent, God heard her laugh because God is everywhere. God asked Abraham, "Why did Sarah laugh?"

Abraham didn't have an answer; he didn't know Sarah had laughed and she didn't know that God had heard her laugh. She didn't even know God had asked Abraham why she had laughed. Then the Lord asked, "Why did you laugh?"

Before Abraham could explain that they were in the presence of God, Sarah answered, "I didn't laugh."

"Not so!" the Lord said to Sarah. "You did laugh, a sarcastic laugh of unbelief."

What could Sarah say? The One who reveals thoughts had told Sarah about her laughter, even when no one heard it. Then He reminded her, "With men this is impossible, but with God nothing is impossible."

There was no discussion that evening of Ishmael, Abraham's son with the Egyptian maid. Even though the blood of Abraham flowed in Ishmael's veins, he was not the son of promise.

The next morning the three travelers said they had to go to Sodom. "You can see the city from here," Abraham told them, "but the trail is difficult to follow." He picked up his walking stick and announced, "I'll go with you to make sure you don't get lost."

Abraham and the three visitors began descending the hill toward Sodom. Soon the other two visitors went on ahead to Sodom. Abraham was left alone in the presence of God. The Lord then began to share with Abraham what He intended to do. "I have heard the cry of the city of Sodom," God told Abraham. What God was going to do was so crucial that He couldn't hide it from Abraham. "The sin of Sodom is so great that I am going to visit the city to determine if I will judge it."

Abraham was grieved at the thought of Sodom's being punished. His married nephew, Lot, had chosen to live in Sodom and had children living in the city. Sodom was a city of commerce . . . multitudes lived there . . . a trade center. Abraham knew Sodom was wicked, so he lived a nomadic life in tents in order to live separately from the people of the cities, as well as from their sins: drunkenness, violence, debauchery, sexual violence. Out in the hills, Abraham could pray to God, and he was surrounded by creation that reminded him of God, the Creator.

Abraham came close to the Lord, dropped to his knees and bowed his face to the ground. "Please, Lord, please don't destroy the city."

Minutes of silence passed between them, as Abraham searched for meaning to his emotions. Then Abraham remembered how he had bargained with other tribal heads, trying to get the other person to meet him halfway. Abraham wondered how many righteous people it would take to save the city, so he dared to ask the Lord, "If you find 50 righteous people in Sodom, if there are 50, will you spare the city?"

God answered Abraham, "If I find 50 righteous people in Sodom, I will not destroy the city."

Abraham began to think of all the good people in Sodom he knew about, and wondered what would happen if the goal of 50 were not met. "Would you save the city if you found only 45?"

God answered, "I will spare Sodom if I find only 45 righteous."

The same thing happened again in Abraham's mind. "Suppose there are not 45 good people in Sodom. Will you save Sodom for 40 righteous souls?"

Abraham had sacrificed to God on a regular basis, he had confessed his sins and prayed to God, but on these occasions he didn't hear the audible voice of God. However, on other occasions, Abraham talked audibly to God. He heard God speak and God carried on a conversation with him, but still he didn't see God. This was different. Now God had visited him. Now he had seen God, talked to God, listened to God, begged God for mercy.

God answered Abraham, "I will spare the city if I find only 40 righteous souls."

The ever-present doubt again popped into Abraham's mind. With great reluctance Abraham again prayed, thinking he was asking too much. "Will you spare the city for 30 righteous souls?"

"I will spare Sodom for 30 righteous souls," a patient God responded to the persistent request of an aging patriarch who was more concerned with people than he was about embarrassing himself before God. And so Abraham repeated the process, asking God to spare the city for 20 righteous people. God agreed.

Abraham realized he knew little about the city of Sodom, but he knew that Lot, his wife, their four daughters and sons-in-law lived there—a total of 10 people. He would make one more request. "If you find only 10 righteous . . . will you spare the city?"

"I will spare the city if I find 10 righteous people."

Abraham stopped at 10; he didn't even think of asking again. Never did he imagine that God couldn't find 10 righteous people in Sodom.

Abraham stopped praying, drew his hands under his body and used them to push himself up off the earth. His joints creaked and his feeble knees were weak, but with effort he was able to stand. He returned home thinking he had saved Sodom. Later he saw the thick yellow smoke of burning sulfur rising from the city, and he realized there had not been 10 righteous to be found there.

Abraham knew the Lord was true to His Word, for His promises to destroy a sensuous city were just as true as His promise that Abraham would have a son. Abraham had sex with his wife, Sarah, and she conceived and gave birth to Isaac. The name Isaac means *laughter*, to remind them both that God keeps His promises. Even when His people laugh in unbelief, God is faithful.

AFTER THE ENCOUNTER

Abraham is the only person in the Bible whom God calls His friend. Because of his faith in God, Abraham walked with God and talked with God. Jesus said, "Abraham rejoiced to see My day" (John 8:56). Jesus was probably referring to the day when Abraham interceded before Him. God kept His promises to Abraham, who became the father of the Jewish nation, with the children of Israel as numerous as the sands of the seashores.

Abraham's Lessons in Finding God

1. *God encounters us at unexpected times.* Abraham didn't expect to see God, at least not this way. When God promised him a son, Abraham did it his way. He took an Egyptian maid, Hagar, and had a son, Ishmael. But Ishmael was not God's promised son through Sarah.

   On the top of a hill, off the beaten path on a hot afternoon, God encountered Abraham. Obviously, Abraham was not expecting God, but he quickly prepared a meal to feed three travelers. Only later did he find out that one of them was a physical manifestation of God, a Christophany, or appearance of Jesus Christ. Later Jesus said, "Your father Abraham rejoiced to see My day, and he saw it and was glad" (John 8:56). Most scholars agree that this encounter with God was actually the experience when Abraham saw Jesus Christ.

YOU HAVE HEDGED ME BEHIND AND BEFORE, AND LAID
YOUR HAND UPON ME. SUCH IS TOO WONDERFUL FOR
ME; IT IS HIGH, I CANNOT ATTAIN IT.

PSALM 139:5,6

2. *God encounters us for a purpose.* It seems that God had a twofold purpose in this encounter. First, God wanted to remind Abraham of the promise that he would have a son; for the first time, God included Sarah in the promise. Her response was not of faith; she laughed in unbelief and was rebuked by God.

The second purpose of this encounter was to tell Abraham about judgment on Sodom. Being a godly man, Abraham immediately interceded before God to save the city and the people of Sodom.

I WILL NOT LEAVE YOU ORPHANS; I WILL COME TO YOU.

JOHN 14:18

3. *God recognizes our statements of unbelief.* There were two responses of laughter. In the previous chapter when God told Abraham that he would have a son, the Bible says, "Abraham fell on his face and laughed" (Gen. 17:17). Abraham's laugh was one of faith; he was glad that God was going to give him a son. However, Sarah's laughter was not of faith; it was motivated by skepticism to express the unbelief of her heart. Even the context of her thoughts describes her vacillation: "Therefore Sarah laughed within herself, saying, 'After I have grown old, shall I have pleasure, my lord being old also?'" (18:12).

God immediately recognized her hard-heartedness and asked, "Why did Sarah laugh?" (v. 13). In grace, God called Sarah to accountability for her laughter. Some of us have laughed at God, or at least been motivated by unbelief, and God leaves us alone. We never realize that we have missed an encounter with Him.

NOW [JESUS] DID NOT DO MANY MIGHTY WORKS
THERE BECAUSE OF THEIR UNBELIEF.
MATTHEW 13:58

4. *Sometimes we lie to God, forgetting there are two persons to whom we cannot lie: God and ourselves.* When the Lord confronted Sarah about her laughter, she denied it out of fear, saying, "I did not laugh" (Gen. 18:15). The Bible teaches that all of us lie (see Ps. 116:11). But there is a certain irony in anyone's attempt to lie, because the one person you can't lie to is yourself; you know the truthfulness of what you are saying. Neither can you lie to God. Because God is Truth, He confronted Sarah with her lie. The most gracious thing God can do for us is to use our consciences to help us correct our problem.

TAKE AWAY MY HABIT OF LYING,
AND GIVE ME A DESIRE TO DO GOD'S LAW.
PSALM 119:29, AUTHOR'S PARAPHRASE

5. *Those who are friends with God know His heart.* Three times in the Bible Abraham is called a friend of God (see 2 Chron. 20:7; Isa. 41:8; Jas. 2:23). No other person in the Bible is called God's friend.

Friends do not hide things from friends, so God opened up His heart and told Abraham what He planned to do in Sodom. And what was Abraham's response? Out of a heart broken for people, Abraham—the friend of God—went into God's presence to intercede for the city and the people.

YOU ARE MY FRIENDS IF YOU DO WHATEVER I COMMAND YOU.

JOHN 15:14

6. *A patient God responds to persistent intercession.* As we see Abraham on his face before God, two qualities are evident. First, the persistence of Abraham in that he didn't stop praying too soon. He began asking for God to save the city if He found 50 righteous people. Then Abraham continued interceding until he got the number down to 10.

The second picture we see is a patient God who allows a human to plead before Him for the souls of others. Rather than being irritated or impatient, God responded to the faith of Abraham as he interceded for the souls in Sodom.

PRAY WITHOUT CEASING.

I THESSALONIANS 5:17

7. *People can influence God when encountering Him.* Usually, we think about God's influence on us when we

encounter Him. But don't forget the opposite is also true, we can influence God. God answers our prayers when our motives are for biblical results, our heart is pure and our faith is strong.

AND WHATEVER YOU ASK IN MY NAME, THAT I WILL DO,
THAT THE FATHER MAY BE GLORIFIED IN THE SON.
JOHN 14:13

Take-Aways

- I can be encountered by God at unexpected times.
- I am encountered by God for a purpose.
- I usually forget that God knows all about me.
- I cannot lie to God.
- I can be God's friend and know Him.
- I can have my prayers heard by God.
- I can influence God in an encounter.

FACE-TO-FACE FIVE TIMES*

JOHN MAXWELL
PASTOR OF TWO DIFFERENT MEGACHURCHES
AND INTERNATIONALLY KNOWN SPEAKER IN
LEADERSHIP TRAINING

FIVE LIFE-CHANGING EXPERIENCES

God stretched me and changed me with five crucial experiences. The principles by which I now live were hammered out on the anvil of these five crises.

The Death of a Friend—and of a Habit

The first crisis was in the early '70s, a time of spiritual formation early in my ministry. The death of a friend changed me from a happy-go-lucky preacher who wanted to be a friend to everyone into a concerned man of God.

At the time, I was with my first church, in Hillhan, Indiana. I began with seven people, and although I moved the congregation forward dramatically in terms of numbers, it was not growing spiritually. During this time, I visited a friend in the hospital repeatedly. Looking back, one of my main drives was to get the patient to like me. Then the friend died. During the funeral, I wept openly—not for the grieving family or friends, but for my own barren spiritual condition.

Over the next year I earnestly sought the Lord, repenting of my spiritual callousness. I remember one Saturday night when I was preparing for a sermon. I was lying under the dining room table, praying with my face to the floor, begging God for true spiritual power. It was not one instantaneous moment that changed my life; but gradually, over a period of months, I became more committed to the spiritual dynamics of pastoring a flock. Like John Wesley, I obtained perfect love and true holiness. I was filled with the Holy Spirit and received power for spiritual witnessing to lead people to Christ.

Expanding Horizons

A second crisis experience happened in February 1973, at a bus conference in Lynchburg, Virginia. Up to this point, because of my ecclesiastical background, I had not been exposed to great evangelistic churches or great evangelistic preaching. At Lynchburg, I saw the great busing ministry at Thomas Road Baptist Church. I heard the testimonies of leaders from massive churches with tremendous evangelistic outreaches. I realized I had limited God by my own unbelief. Under the ministry of Wally Beebe, Jerry Falwell, Bob Gray and others, I realized that I needed to expand my horizons.

Back in my room at the Holiday Inn, I wrestled with God all night. Lying on the floor again, I made a commitment to double my church in Lancaster in one year. The church was averaging 400 in attendance, and I determined to have an additional 400 on the buses within one year. I also committed to go back and publicly announce my new determination to my church.

Upon returning to Ohio, I rallied the people to begin the following Saturday knocking on doors to invite people to ride a bus to Sunday School. On Sunday morning the bus pulled up to the church and 19 children got off. I remember hugging everyone in the church foyer as we counted the children. "Since we had 19 children on the bus," I announced, "we can use our other bus and get 38 next Sunday." And we did. Within a year we had reached our goal of averaging as many on the buses as in worship attendance. When I began to think big and not limit God, the people began to think big and not limit God.

The Barren Altar

The third crisis happened in November 1973, at a Sword of the Lord conference under the ministry of John R. Rice. I was convicted about the "barren altar"—the lack of conversions at my church. I wrestled with God in the car all the way home. I prayed, "Lord, let there never be a Sunday when people are not saved at the church." Big attendance was not enough. Upon my return, I again announced to my congregation that in the following year we would do all we could not to have a barren altar, but to make it a great year of soul-winning.

During that year, I invited Elmer Towns to preach for me at the church. Since it was the weekend of the Towns's anniversary, I invited him to bring his wife, and we would join them for their anniversary dinner. When Towns arrived, I told him that it was visitation night, and I had made a commitment to go soul-winning. Even though there was social pressure on me to keep my commitment to Dr. Towns, that evening I visited a lawyer named John Polston and won him to the Lord. For the next several years when Towns visited the church to preach, Polston would remind us how happy he was that I had gone soul-winning that night instead of going out for an anniversary dinner.

In 1974, I made a goal personally to win 200 people to Christ. A great sense of revival broke out among the people when I made that announcement. I did not quite reach my goal that year, but I did lead 186 to pray to receive Christ. I feel this established the credibility of soul-winning among the church members, and established the foundation for all of the changes in the church, including constructing new buildings and instituting new ministries.

Networking and Praying

The fourth experience was not so much a crisis as it was a number of rich conversations with successful pastors. I phoned several great pastors and offered them 100 dollars each for an hour of their time in order to discover the reasons why their churches had done so well. As I visited and talked with these outstanding leaders, I asked them to pray with me. And after each interview, I went to my car, bowed my head over the steering wheel and asked for spiritual strength to build a great church.

A Crisis of Glory

The fifth experience occurred when I received the award for having the fastest-growing Sunday School in Ohio in 1976. The award, a large banner, was presented by Christian Life magazine at the International Christian Education Convention in Detroit, Michigan. The Sunday School at the Lancaster church had grown from an average weekly attendance of 860 to 1,012.

After the award ceremony, I returned to my hotel and again lying on my face, laid the banner out before God. At that moment, I realized that I had been honored for doing only what I *should* do, for growth was what every church *ought* to do. I opened the Scriptures and reread the words of Jesus in Matthew 16:18: "I will build my church." The church belongs to Jesus, not to John Maxwell. It is God who is to be honored, not men. In the midst of this crisis, I decided to give God the glory for everything in my ministry. That night I realized I was gifted to serve the Lord, and that God must get the credit for any gift because "Every good . . . gift is from above" (Jas. 1:17).

---

* Elmer Towns, *10 of Today's Most Innovative Churches* (Ventura, CA: Regal Books, 1990), pp. 23-26.

CHAPTER 2

JACOB:
SEEING GOD FACE-TO-FACE

ENCOUNTER: OUT OF FEAR

PLACE: IN A TENT NEAR THE JABBOK RIVER

SCRIPTURE: GENESIS 31:11-32; 32:1-32

The two men stared defiantly at each other, a large jagged rock in the middle of the road separating them from physical assault. The older of the two men, Laban, had chased down his foe and caught him at this rock. His clenched hands were unarmed, but his dedicated servants had their weapons ready: swords, bows and spears. A dozen mean-spirited, dirty and tired men had followed their angry master, and now they were willing to fight at his word. But their aging leader stood silent.

The hot desert wind whipped up sand around their ankles, their tunics flapping around their bodies. The blistering sun burnt their tempers raw. A dirty beard and foul-smelling clothes from a hard chase didn't help old Laban's disposition.

The younger Jacob stared from the other side of the stone at his uncle and father-in-law, Laban. Neither man trusted the other. If anyone had lurched for a weapon, there would have been a battle. Laban's two dozen warriors had worked in the fields with Jacob, and they didn't trust him; they were ready to kill him. Jacob had as many herdsmen as Laban to tend his large flocks. They were not warriors, but they knew if a battle began they would have to fight for their lives.

Silence, except for the hot wind.

"Why did you take my daughters?" Laban's raspy voice finally broke the tension. "Why did you sneak off into the night with my grandchildren?"

"I knew you wouldn't let me go," Jacob sheepishly answered. For the first time he dropped his eyes in guilt.

"They are my daughters." Laban's voice got more powerful. "These are my children." He waved to make sure everyone knew he was referring to the 11 sons of Jacob. "You have gotten rich from my flock." Laban pointed to the several flocks of animals milling around: goats, rams, camels, cows, bulls and donkeys. They were the sign of wealth, and Laban suspected Jacob had stolen much from him.

"Let this rock," Laban said as he pointed for all to see the gouged boulder in the middle of the road, "be a division between us. You will not come on this side of the rock . . . and I will not come on your side."

"Agreed," Jacob quickly shouted for all to hear. "I agree!"

"Bring a knife," Laban demanded.

At first, Jacob flinched when he heard the word "knife," but then he remembered the nomadic tradition. Laban grabbed the knife, quickly pierced his wrist until blood appeared and then threw the knife over the rock to Jacob. Jacob followed his uncle's example. Then reaching out, they clasped hands to arms, the blood of one relative mingling with the other. Together they agreed by blood . . . blood touching blood. Together they said,

"May the Lord watch between you and me, while we are separated one from the other."

Laban kissed his daughters and children. Then as he prepared to mount his horse, he again pointed to the rock. "This rock is my witness; I will not cross to your side." He stopped his words in midsentence and then turned and pointed to Jacob. "If you hurt one of my children, God is witness to what I will do."

With that warning Laban turned abruptly, still angry but now somewhat pacified, and dug his heels into the side of his horse. As he bolted down the road, his warriors fell into columns, following Laban eastward toward home.

All that day and the next, the words of Laban haunted Jacob. Even though his uncle promised not to pass the stone—he called the stone Mizpah—Jacob couldn't be sure that his uncle would not attack in the night, killing him and taking his daughters and grandchildren.

While the memory of an angry uncle terrified Jacob, it also reminded him of his brother, Esau. Twenty years earlier, Jacob had sneaked out of his father's tent because Esau had threatened him: "When Father is dead, I will kill you."

Jacob saw his brother's anger and believed Esau would kill him, so he had run away from home. He had spent those 20 years with his Uncle Laban, marrying two of Laban's daughters, Leah and Rachel. Now Jacob was going home. He was a wealthy man: 2 wives, 11 sons, servants, herds of cattle. He had left empty; now he led a large nomadic tribe toward the Promised Land. He was leaving an angry uncle and heading toward an angry brother.

Jacob had tricked his older brother out of the birthright, which meant Jacob became the family head, the family spokesman, the family priest. Next Jacob had tricked Esau out of the blessing. Jacob's father had promised him twice as much inheritance as his brother, only he never got any; instead, he ran, fearing for his life.

Early the next morning, Jacob sent servants to Esau, with directions on how to find his brother. "Call Esau 'my master.' Tell him I'm returning home . . . tell him how rich I am . . . tell him I want to find grace in his eyes."

Jacob waited two days for their return. He prayed to the Lord, asking for grace. God had appeared to him 20 years earlier and promised several things: I am the Lord God of your fathers, Abraham and Isaac. I will give this land to you and to your children. You will have many children. I will make you rich. I will protect you (see Gen. 28:13-15).

It was that last part about protection that Jacob was counting on as he prayed. Suddenly, his thoughts were interrupted by shouts outside the tent: "The servants are returning!"

The two servants who had been to Esau went directly to Jacob's tent. Jacob had been praying for a friendly message, but the message Jacob heard from his servants was worse than his deepest fears: "Esau is coming to meet you with 400 armed men."

There was no place to run, no place to hide. He couldn't return to Laban; the Mizpah rock stood in the middle of the road. Panic seized Jacob and it was difficult to think, but slowly a plan developed in his mind. "I'll give Esau everything. Maybe then he won't kill me."

Jacob was quick witted; he could always scramble out of trouble. He was Jacob the supplanter, Jacob the trickster. His scheme to give Esau everything was an elaborate plan, designed to confuse his brother.

Jacob separated his flocks into several divisions, putting servants over each flock and keeping the flocks separate from one another. Jacob then started the flocks journeying toward Esau, one flock at a time, each flock just out of sight of the other. First,

> 200 she goats . . . next,
> 200 he goats . . . next,
> 200 ewes . . . next,
> 200 rams . . . next,
> 30 milk cows . . . next,
> 40 cattle for meat . . . next,
> 10 bulls . . . next,
> 20 female donkeys . . . next,
> 10 young donkeys.

Jacob told his herdsmen they would recognize Esau by his red beard, and he instructed them to bow to the ground and say to him, "This is a present to you from your servant Jacob, who is coming behind us."

Nine times that day the same thing would happen. Esau would see a cloud of dust approaching. Each time Esau would think the dust might be an approaching army, and each time, he would prepare for battle. Each time Esau would draw his sword, and each time his men would follow Esau's example. But each time Jacob tricked him, as Esau received another gift from his returning brother. As the number of gifts grew, Esau began to think Jacob must be very wealthy indeed.

All of the herds did not reach Esau before nightfall. Esau camped for the night, surrounded by the moans of the cattle and the bleating of sheep. "Tomorrow I'll see my brother Jacob," he mused, as the redheaded Esau tried to sleep. "Tomorrow will climax 20 years of agony."

Jacob camped for the evening near the small river Jabbok, still up to his old tricks. He pitched his big tent on the riverbank and entered with his two wives and children. The servants were dispatched to sleep on the ground around the tent. The fires were to burn throughout the night. If Esau attacked during the night, he would capture the wives, the children and the servants; but he would not capture Jacob, who had one last trick up his sleeve.

As soon as darkness surrounded the massive tent, Jacob sneaked out from under the flaps. No one saw him, not the servants, nor his family. The moonless night painted dark shadows, and it was easy to escape from the camp unseen. He waded across the shallow Jabbok River, where he found the small tent he had hidden in a small cluster of trees. Once inside, he knelt to pray, as wild thoughts raced through his mind. "Will Uncle Laban return to kill me . . . or will my brother Esau kill me tomorrow?"

Jacob knelt before God, bowing his face to the ground. "O God of my grandfather, Abraham . . . O God of my father, Isaac . . . I am returning to my country because You are sending me home," Jacob prayed, reminding God that he was being obedient to the vision God had given him to return to his home country. Jacob confessed his sins and held his prized walking stick up to God. "I only had this staff when I crossed Jordan 20 years ago." Tears of gratitude came to his eyes. "You have blessed me with a family . . . with children . . . with flocks . . . with servants. Tonight I am divided from my family."

Lonely. Twenty years earlier Jacob left his father and mother because he had deceived his family. Lonely. That night he prepared to reenter the Promised Land. Lonely. He had once again deceived his family.

"Deliver me from my brother, Esau, because I fear he will kill me and the children, and their mothers." Jacob could not bear the thought of no sons, no seed to Abraham's promise, God's promises cut off. "Lord, You promised to do me good," Jacob reminded God. "You promised I would have more children than the sand of the seashore."

Suddenly, Jacob heard the unmistakable crunch of footsteps in the sand outside the tent. *What's that?* he thought, but couldn't speak. He listened as the sounds of steps ceased. Silence! Then the steps began again.

His eyes dilated, his heart rate doubled. He yelled, "Who's there?"

No one answered. The tent flap moved. Jacob saw a hand pull back the flap, and a figure entered the tent. "No," yelled Jacob, jumping up to grab the figure. The two men wrestled to the ground as Jacob reached for the man's arms, holding them lest he have a weapon.

"Release me," the man demanded.

"No," Jacob answered.

Almost immediately Jacob realized the man didn't have a weapon. It was strength against strength, will against will, stamina against stamina. The man was persistent, but of all the things Jacob knew about himself, Jacob knew he was stubborn.

"I have come to answer your prayers," the man said, but the trickster thought he knew better.

"How do I know you have come from God?" Jacob grunted.

"You are afraid of being killed," the opponent answered.

"That's easy to see. I'm hiding in this tent because I'm afraid."

"You've asked God to protect you," the opponent said.

"All my servants have heard me pray that," Jacob sneered, continuing to hold on because that was the way he lived and fought. He knew if he let go, he would lose. "If you're from God . . . if God sent you, then bless me."

They wrestled for hours. The moon never rose to let Jacob see his enemy. Through the black night he wrestled an unseen figure, one stronger than he. Jacob had finally met a person he couldn't beat or trick. All he could do was hang on.

Then the first light of a new day peeked over an eastern hill. "Let me go," the figure demanded, "for the dawn is breaking."

"No!" Jacob repeated the answer he had given all night. "I will not let you go except you bless me."

"What is your name?" the figure asked.

"Jacob," he answered, knowing the name meant supplanter, one who deceives.

"You will have a new name," the man told Jacob. "God will bless you. Your name will be 'Israel.' Your new name means 'Prince with God.' You will be special to God for the rest of your life, and God will bless your children who will continue forever, because you have wrestled with God and would not let go, because you have always sought the Lord, in spite of your deception, because you have prevailed."

The figure touched Jacob's thigh, and a pain shot down his leg to his toes and then up his nervous system into his brain. He screamed in agony.

"You will limp for the rest of your life," Jacob heard the voice say. "Everywhere you walk, you will walk with pain and you will remember this night; you will remember that you wrestled with God and would not let go."

"Tell me your name," Jacob said as his pain subsided.

"Why do you want to know my name?" he answered. "You don't need to know my name! But you have prayed to God for His blessing, and I will bless you."

Jacob realized this person had heard his prayers, and only God can hear the prayers of men. This person had known his heart, and only God knows the hearts of men. This person was going to bless him, and only God can give blessings.

Jacob knelt before the figure, the experience of pain in his thigh compensated by the awesome experience of God's presence. Jacob bowed his head, afraid to look up. Even though he could see traces of the man's face in the early morning light, Jacob was afraid to look. He was ashamed of his unbelief throughout the previous night.

The hand touched Jacob with God's blessing, and Jacob would never be the same. He had touched God and been touched by God. From then on he would walk with God, no longer relying on his human escapades. Jacob would be Israel—a Prince with God.

Jacob emerged from the small tent, the piercing sun now shining over the eastern hill through the white birch trees. "I have seen God," Jacob said, though no one was present to hear him. "I have seen God face-to-face and did not die."

As Jacob took a step toward the Jabbok River, pain shot through his hip, stopping him short. He reached back into the tent for his walking stick and hobbled down to the Jabbok River to wash himself and to take a drink of cool water to revive his spirit.

"I'll name this place Peniel, face of God," Jacob declared. "For this is where I saw God face-to-face."

Jacob had asked for God's hand of protection; instead, he had met Him face-to-face.

AFTER THE ENCOUNTER

Jacob, the one who schemed and lied, became Israel, a Prince with God. He became a man of faith and directed his 12 sons—through whom came the 12 tribes—in worship and obedience of God. He limped for the rest of his life, which reminded him of his encounter with God.

Jacob's Lessons in Encountering God

1. *Different motivations drive us to seek God.* Jacob was running *from* an angry uncle and *towards* an angry brother. Because of his fear, Jacob sought God alone in a tent. But something happened in that tent that changed his life. Once he encountered God, Jacob wouldn't let Him go. The constant thing in Jacob's life prior to this experience was to hang on, so what Jacob always did in the past became the source of changing his life. Whatever your motivation—fear, bankruptcy, IRS audit, cancer, divorce—whatever motivates you to seek God, when you get into His presence, hang on to Him. His intimacy will change your life.

WHENEVER I AM AFRAID, I WILL TRUST IN YOU.

PSALM 56:3

2. *Concerns for family drive us into God's presence.* Jacob had wives and children; he constantly prayed for their safety. While his own life was his greatest concern, his prayer for his family was utmost on his lips. When God can't get our attention any other way, He reaches us through our spouse or children. He can even use family arguments to cause us to seek Him, as He did with Jacob in his hostile relationships with Laban and Esau.

WHEN MY FATHER AND MY MOTHER FORSAKE ME,

THEN THE LORD WILL TAKE CARE OF ME.

PSALM 27:10

3. *We must give up precious things of life to encounter God's presence.* Jacob gave up everything. He was willing to surrender all his cattle to Esau; he was willing to sacrifice his family; he offered to God the only thing he brought out of the Promised Land, the only thing that went everywhere with him—he surrendered his walking stick to God. Only then did Jacob experience God's presence. If you are going to encounter intimacy with God, you must not let anything come between you and God.

HE WHO LOVES FATHER OR MOTHER MORE THAN ME IS NOT WORTHY OF ME. AND HE WHO LOVES SON OR DAUGHTER MORE THAN ME IS NOT WORTHY OF ME. AND HE WHO DOES NOT TAKE HIS CROSS AND FOLLOW AFTER ME IS NOT WORTHY OF ME. HE WHO FINDS HIS LIFE WILL LOSE IT, AND HE WHO LOSES HIS LIFE FOR MY SAKE WILL FIND IT.
MATTHEW 10:37-39

4. *When everything seems lost, seek God's face.* Jacob thought he was about to lose everything. He even thought the footsteps outside his tent were those of an avenger. His greatest terror was the fear in his own heart. When all seemed lost, God came to him because Jacob, in desperation, sought God's face. God allows us to experience the extremities of our hearts, because man's extremities are God's opportunities. It is in these desperate experiences that God reveals Himself to us.

BUT AS FOR ME, MY FEET HAD ALMOST STUMBLED; MY STEPS HAD NEARLY SLIPPED. NEVERTHELESS I AM

CONTINUALLY WITH YOU; YOU HOLD ME BY MY RIGHT
HAND. YOU WILL GUIDE ME WITH YOUR COUNSEL, AND
AFTERWARD RECEIVE ME TO GLORY. WHOM HAVE I IN
HEAVEN BUT YOU? AND THERE IS NONE UPON EARTH
THAT I DESIRE BESIDES YOU.
PSALM 73:2, 23-25

5. *Seeking God is something you must do alone.* Jacob's wives or
children couldn't help him seek God's presence. Laban
and Esau were not able to help him spiritually. Jacob
wrestled alone with God and prevailed. He saw God face-
to-face. You can't wait for your spouse to go with you in
your journey to God. It is a lonesome journey, and it's a
journey you take by yourself. As Abraham interceded
alone for Sodom, as Moses interceded alone on Sinai, as
Elijah alone stood against 450 prophets of Baal on Mount
Carmel, as George Washington knelt alone in the snow
of Valley Forge, so you must seek God's face alone.

WAIT ON THE LORD: BE OF GOOD COURAGE,
AND HE SHALL STRENGTHEN THINE HEART:
WAIT, I SAY, ON THE LORD.
PSALM 27:14, *KJV*

6. *We are usually surprised by an encounter with God.* Jacob
didn't expect God's presence in the tent. He retreated
there to hide. Jacob didn't expect to wrestle all night
with God. Would he have held on to the figure if he
had known it was God? Could he have let go if he had
known it was God? Jacob was surprised to find himself
in God's presence. Sometimes we go to church, never

expecting to meet God, but even in the unusual and unexpected places, we are surprised by God.

WHEN MY HEART IS OVERWHELMED; LEAD ME TO THE
ROCK THAT IS HIGHER THAN I.
PSALM 61:2

7. *After the blackest experiences at the lowest times of life, the dawn comes where we understand our encounter with God in the valley.* Sometimes God doesn't come to us when everything is rosy. When we have health, happiness, money in the bank and no threats, we usually don't think much about God. But the blackest nights scare us because we can't see where we're going, we can't see things, we can't see ourselves, nor can we see God. In those black experiences, we can seek God and He will reveal Himself to us.

For several days, Jacob lived in a dark valley that became progressively blacker. The more Jacob manipulated circumstances, the worse they became. Only in the blackest experiences did Jacob meet God and eventually receive God's blessing. When we come to the end of our way, we need to turn to God. He will come to us. There always is a bright shining morning that follows the storms of the night.

WEEPING MAY ENDURE FOR A NIGHT, BUT JOY COMES IN
THE MORNING. YOU HAVE TURNED FOR ME MY MOURN-
ING INTO DANCING; YOU HAVE PUT OFF MY SACKCLOTH
AND CLOTHED ME WITH GLADNESS.
PSALM 30:5,11

Take-Aways

- I can seek God for different reasons.
- I can seek God because I am concerned for my family.
- I must give up prized things to encounter God.
- I can seek God when everything seems lost.
- I will seek God by myself.
- I am usually surprised when God encounters me.
- I can expect the dawn after the blackest night.

THE COURAGE FROM GOD*

BILLY GRAHAM
EVANGELIST

In my own life there have been times when I have also had the sense of being filled with the Spirit, knowing that some special strength was added for some task I was being called upon to perform.

We sailed for England in 1954 for a crusade that was to last for three months. While on the ship, I experienced a definite sense of oppression. Satan seemed to have assembled a formidable array of his artillery against me. Not only was I oppressed, I was overtaken by a sense of depression, accompanied by a frightening feeling of inadequacy for the task that lay ahead. Almost night and day I prayed. I knew in a new way what Paul was telling us when he spoke about "praying without ceasing." Then one day in a prayer meeting with my wife and colleagues, a break came. As I wept before the Lord, I was filled with deep assurance that power belonged to God and He was faithful. I had been baptized by the Spirit into the Body of Christ when I was saved, but I believe God gave me a special anointing on the way to England. From that moment on I was confident that God the Holy Spirit was in control for the task that lay ahead.

That proved true.

Experiences of this kind had happened to me before, and they have happened to me many times since. Sometimes no tears are shed. Sometimes as I have lain awake at night the quiet assurance has come that I was being filled with the Spirit for the task that lay ahead.

However, there have been many more occasions when I would have to say as the apostle Paul did in I Corinthians 2:3: "I was with you in weakness, in fear and in much trembling." Frequently various members of my team have assured me that when I have had the least liberty in preaching or the greatest feeling of failure, God's power has been most evident.

---

*   Elmer Towns, *Understanding the Deeper Life* (Old Tappan, NJ: Revell, 1988), pp. 214, 215.

CHAPTER 3

MOSES:
THE SERVANT OF GOD

ENCOUNTER: OUT OF FRUSTRATION
PLACE: MOUNT SINAI IN THE WILDERNESS
SCRIPTURE: EXODUS 32:1—34:35

The ragged mountain peak itself was a problem, as much as all the other problems Moses faced. The mountain was tall—7,550 feet in elevation—the mountain was steep, the paths were treacherous, with lurking serpents and dangerous cliffs. Moses faced physical barriers. He was over 80 years old. Some thought he was too frail to make it to the top and return. As he began his journey, a voice had yelled from the mixed multitude, "Moses will die on Mount Sinai!"

The voice didn't frighten Moses; it was the people who faced danger. They had been warned to stay away from the mountain; any person or animal that strayed onto the mountain would die. Fathers retreated to wait in their tent doors; mothers had gathered up their children to flee inside their tents out of fear. The smell of death drifted over the entire camp of Israel. Those rebellious Jews who had polluted themselves by dancing naked before the idolatrous golden bull were dead.

Moses paused to catch his breath. The path was steep and his old legs were tired.

After a few minutes of rest, he continued his climb. It was slow because his muscles had weakened over the years. He pulled hard on his staff each time he climbed over a large stone. He pushed himself over the rocks with his rod, the one he called "the rod of God."

Again, Moses stopped to rest and think. He remembered throwing down the rod and it became a serpent; he remembered stretching out the rod and the Red Sea parted; he remembered hitting the rock and out came water.

"No miracles today," Moses said to himself. Yesterday had been a tough day. Yesterday, Moses had to deal with the sin of Israel. Yesterday was the worst day in the history of Israel. Yesterday when Moses came down from Sinai, he heard people shouting; he mistakenly thought there was a battle. But Israel had lost its moral senses. The people were dancing naked; some were bowing before a golden bull to worship it. The people had turned their backs on the leadership of Moses; they had repudiated God.

Yesterday the ringleaders perished because of their rebellion against God. Yesterday Moses ran as fast as his old legs would carry him toward the Tabernacle, yelling to the people as he went, "You have sinned a great sin! But I will make intercession for you. Perhaps God will not destroy all of us." Moses rushed boldly into the holy of holies to intercede for the nation of Israel.

Yesterday he spread himself out on his face before God, before the Ark of the Covenant. With tears wetting his long, stringy beard, Moses begged God, "Oh, this people have sinned a great sin. Forgive their sins."

Yesterday Moses pleaded many times until God interrupted him. "Let Me alone. These people are stiff-necked and rebellious.

My anger burns against them for what they did."

Moses wept at the words of God. "Please forgive them," he begged.

But God was determined to destroy Israel. The Lord's voice could be heard throughout the large tent—the Tabernacle—where God dwelt. "I will blot out these people. I will begin a new nation through you."

Moses didn't want to be the father of a new nation. Abraham was the father of Israel. Israel had a wonderful heritage of Isaac, Jacob, Joseph and the elders in Egypt. Moses prayed to God, reminding Him of the miracles that delivered Israel out of bondage, and of His promises to the faithful patriarchs. "These people are Your people. You have delivered them from Egypt. Remember Abraham, Isaac and Israel, Your servants. The Egyptians will laugh at You for bringing Your people into the wilderness to destroy them."

Yesterday the black cloud of God's presence had settled over the Tabernacle. The presence of God had visited His tent to listen to the prayers of His servant Moses. They talked for a long time. Finally, Moses put his whole life on the line for Israel. "If you can't forgive their sins, blot me out of Your book."

The heart of God is broken over the sin of His people, but more than that, the heart of God responds to the intercession of His servants. In tenderness God told Moses, "I will forgive their sins . . ."

Moses prevailed. God forgave their sins; Israel would not die. But because of their transgression, God added a condition to His blessing them. God told Moses to lead the people to the Promised Land, but things would not be the same in the future as they had been in the past. God told Moses that He would not go with them. Instead, He said, "I will send the Angel of the Lord to lead you . . ."

That was yesterday in the valley; today Moses was going to the top of Sinai to meet God. Today was a new day.

Moses looked down the mountain on the tents of Israel. In the center of the camp, he saw the Tabernacle. Suddenly, a heavy wet cloud drifted toward Moses and almost immediately enveloped him. He could no longer see down the mountain to the tents of Israel on the desert floor, nor could he look up to see the top of Sinai. He realized this was not an average cloud, as he felt the presence of God. This was the thick cloud in which God dwelt.

Moses spread his robe on the ground before him, dropped to his knees and waited a moment, listening for God's voice. All he could hear was the rustle of a slight breeze in the underbrush. There were no trees at this height on Sinai. He looked for words to express his feelings. "Lord God, You have let me bring these people out of Egypt, but You have said You will not go with us."

Moses wanted more than an angel to guide him to the Promised Land. He prayed, "Lord God, You know my name. You know I am unfit to be a leader of Your people. If I have found grace in Your sight, You must go with us." Then Moses' voice broke with tears of regret. "Because these are Your people, go with us!"

Moses knew God heard him because he felt the presence of God in that cloud. He knew God heard prayers no matter where they were made, because God is everywhere. Moses also knew that Sinai was special to God. It was on this mountain that Moses saw the burning bush. It was on this mountain that Moses received the Ten Commandments. Because Moses had previously felt the presence of God on this mountain, he continued to pray. "If Your presence does not go with me, don't carry us to the Promised Land."

God answered from the dark cloud, "I will go with you." God had heard Moses' request. He had forgiven His people and restored them to their favored position.

Most would have thought that Moses had just gotten the greatest answer to prayer in his life, and that should be enough. But Moses went on to ask for something more. "Show me Your glory."

"No man can see God and live," God answered.

The top of Sinai was covered with a black cloud, darker than any thundercloud Moses had ever experienced. Moses was in the presence of God. The cloud was thick black smoke—as thick as black mud, as thick as clouded olive oil, as thick as blood. But Moses had moved beyond fear. He had confronted the thieves and wild beasts of his shepherd days and lived. He had confronted Pharaoh, the most powerful man on earth, and lived. Now Moses was in the presence of God—talking to Him, listening to Him, waiting for Him. He had seen God's power. He had seen death. Now Moses wanted to see God.

Then God told Moses what He would do. "I will make my goodness pass before you. I will proclaim My name before you, because when you know My name, you know Me." God told Moses that He would be gracious to whom He would be gracious, and He would show mercy on whom He chose. Then God included Moses in His blessing. "I will show mercy to you. Come, there is a place where you can see My glory."

God led Moses to the top of Sinai. He took Moses to a great rock, a rock taller than a house, wider than a clump of bay trees that spread their branches. The rock was the very top of Sinai, a split rock, like a loaf of bread split by a knife. The split from the top of the rock to the bottom was just large enough to hide a man from sight.

"There," God instructed Moses. "Hide in the crevice of the rock."

A sense of dread overcame Moses; death sat on his shoulder to laugh at him. "I'll die," Moses screamed.

"No," God assured him. "My presence will pass before you, but you'll not die."

The God of heaven prepared to pass in review before the top of Sinai. The God of light who lives in a cloud of thick blackness was poised to do what He said. Sinai was covered with night. Down on the desert floor, the Israelites saw the display of a ferocious lightning storm on Sinai. All the families of Israel retreated into their tents. Flaps were secured as they huddled in fear.

The presence of God moved toward the split rock where Moses was hiding. Then, in an act of mercy, God reached out His hand to cover the crevice in the rock. The glory of God did not consume Moses. The hand of God protected Moses' life. The glory of God roared by as a tornado in its path, only more powerful. The glory of God flowed by silently as a great river, only more forcefully. The glory of God was felt, as a mother's tenderness influences everything in a room. The majesty of God was on parade, and as when a king passes by, observers see nothing else but the sovereign awesomeness of the king.

Moses huddled in the cleft of the rock. He cared not how the rock was split but only that he felt safety inside the huge pierced area. He was hidden behind the hand of God, as the glory of God passed by. Then Moses heard God's powerful voice: "The Lord . . . the Lord God . . . merciful . . . gracious . . . longsuffering . . . abundant in goodness and truth. The Lord keeps mercy for thousands . . . forgiving iniquity . . . but the Lord will visit the iniquity of the unrepentant father on his children unto the third and fourth generation."

The glory of the Lord is the name of the Lord. Moses encountered God's presence on the top of Sinai.

The loud voice of the Lord grew silent, as one hears a voice gently fading as the speaker walks away, singing as he goes. The voice got more faint as the distance grew greater. Then God removed His hand and Moses saw the backside of God in the thick black cloud moving down the valley. Moses felt the intimate presence of God, even though it was receding. Then, straining his eyes to see, Moses could barely make out the form in the thick cloud. What was it?

That's when he understood that it was the backside of God.

Moses stayed on Sinai for 40 days, talking to God, fasting in His presence, hungering and thirsting only after God's righteousness.

Once again, God gave Moses the Ten Commandments. The first time God wrote the Ten Commandments with His finger. This time God spoke, and Moses chiseled them on stone tablets. Moses talked to God and God talked to Moses.

After 40 days, Moses slowly began his descent down the mountain. His walk was more difficult than ever before. Not only was Moses old, but he had just fasted for 40 days. In addition, the stone commandments were heavy. After a torturous trip, Moses saw the tents of Israel between two small hills.

As Moses appeared between the two hills, the watch spotted him. Aaron, Moses' brother, had posted men to watch for Moses. While Moses was enveloped in the thick cloud at the top of Sinai, all Israel had prayed. Most of them stayed in their tents, leaving only for essential requirements. Everyone felt the threat of death about the camp. Each wondered where judgment would next strike. Many thought Moses died on the mountain. To them the thick cloud resembled a fierce thunderstorm. They were sure that the frail old man would perish in the elements. Without Moses to lead them, a few wanted to break camp to head back to Egypt. When the watchers saw Moses descending the mountain, they yelled out toward the camp, "Moses . . . Moses is coming!"

And then they saw it. The face of Moses was shining, like sunlight glistening off a lake.

The hushed crowd stood silently gawking, doubting. Some mothers rounded up their children and herded them into their tents. They couldn't be too careful. They had never before seen a man's face shine.

Moses hadn't known his face glistened. When someone stands in the light, they forget the experience of darkness. Moses had been in the presence of God, and now his face shone.

Aaron and the other leaders backed away as Moses approached them. They covered their faces with upheld arms.

Taking a scarf, Moses hid his face from the people. Then the people cautiously approached their leader. Fear of the unknown makes people shun even those they love.

For the next 40 days Moses' face shone—for the same length of time he fasted in God's presence—and he kept a veil over his face. When he went into the Tabernacle to pray, Moses removed the veil to talk with God, but he put it back on when talking with the people.

AFTER THE ENCOUNTER

After Moses met with God on Mount Sinai, God did not destroy His people but He did lead them into the Promised Land. Moses gave the people the Ten Commandments and established the nation. He set up the Tabernacle and established a code of laws for their spiritual, social, economic and family life. Moses is one of the most revered leaders in the history of Israel.

What Moses' Encounter with God Reveals

1. *Encountering God has physical results.* The face of Moses shone for 40 days because he saw the backside of God. No one can imagine what would have happened if Moses had seen the front side of God. And no one can explain how it happened that his face shone. All we can say is that Moses saw the glory of God and his face reflected God's radiance. As a mirror reflects a candle, as the moon reflects the sun, Moses reflected the glory of God that he had seen.

   When you encounter God, there will be physical results. Some who encounter God are healed of cancer, some receive a miraculous supply of money, some get spiritual power for service. We cannot tell what God will do physically when we encounter Him, because God will do what He chooses to do.

MOSES DID NOT KNOW THAT THE SKIN OF HIS FACE
SHONE WHILE HE TALKED WITH HIM.
EXODUS 34:29

2. *There are geographical locations where God desires to encounter people.* Technically, God can meet people anywhere, and the history of mankind shows that He has done just that. However, there seem to be places where God manifests Himself more than others. The altar was one of those places. God met a person at the entrance to the Tabernacle/Temple when a repentant sinner brought a blood sacrifice to atone for sins.

Obviously, Sinai was another place God delighted to reveal Himself. It was there that Moses saw the burning bush, received the Ten Commandments and saw the glory of God. Later, Elijah would encounter God on that same mountain.

Because of this principle, God met His people at Bethel, Shiloh, Mizpah or any place they sacrificed to Him. Today many churches have an altar at the front of the auditorium where people come for dedication, salvation, healing or just to meet God there. God has encountered people at the altar of a camp meeting, revival meeting or after a Sunday morning worship service.

Today you can encounter God anyplace; but when you need Him, need Him right away, need Him badly, then go back to the place where He likes to work; go back to where you previously met Him. Revisit the place at camp or at church where you dedicated your life to God. If you can't do it physically, revisit it in your mind. If you met God there previously, you can encounter Him there again.

MOSES LED THE FLOCK TO THE BACKSIDE OF THE DESERT
AND CAME TO THE MOUNTAIN PEAK OF SINAI, IN THE
HOREB RANGE, THE MOUNTAIN OF GOD.
EXODUS 3:1, AUTHOR'S PARAPHRASE

3. *The presence of God is linked to the name of God.* When Moses prayed to see the presence of God, it was the name of God that passed in front of him. How can we

get the presence of God in our lives? The Early Church learned that there was forgiveness in the name of Christ, healing in the name of Christ and power in the name of Christ. Demons quaked before that name, and martyrs willingly laid down their lives for that name. You cannot get more of God's presence than you can through His name.

I WILL MAKE ALL MY GOODNESS PASS BEFORE YOU, AND I WILL PROCLAIM THE NAME OF THE LORD BEFORE YOU. I WILL BE GRACIOUS TO WHOM I WILL BE GRACIOUS, AND I WILL HAVE COMPASSION ON WHOM I WILL HAVE COMPASSION.

EXODUS 33:19

4. *Our passion is God Himself, not an angel or any human help.* Moses did something very few intercessors have done . . . he stayed in God's presence until God gave him his request. God told Israel His presence would not go with them into the Promised Land. That was intolerable. Moses prayed fervently and continually until God said He would go with Israel. Too many of us settle for the power of God, the blessing of God or the work of God in our lives. What we need is God Himself.

AND THE LORD SAID TO MOSES. . . . "BEHOLD, MY ANGEL SHALL GO BEFORE YOU." THEN [MOSES] SAID TO [THE LORD], "IF YOUR PRESENCE DOES NOT GO WITH US, DO NOT BRING US UP FROM HERE."

EXODUS 32:33,34; 33:15

5. *We encounter God on His terms, not ours.* Even though Moses begged to see God's glory, he didn't see God the way he expected. Perhaps Moses didn't understand the dangers of getting too close to God. Moses didn't get to see the face of God as he asked, and Moses was placed in a split in the rock to protect him. Even then, God had to cover Moses with His hand, in all probability to save his life.

When we encounter God, it will be on His terms, not ours. He is the giver of that blessing; we are simply the recipients.

AND [MOSES] SAID, "PLEASE, SHOW ME YOUR GLORY."
BUT [THE LORD] SAID, "YOU CANNOT SEE MY FACE;
FOR NO MAN SHALL SEE ME, AND LIVE."
EXODUS 33:18,20

6. *God knows those who encounter Him.* When Moses went into the presence of God, he found out that God knew his name; but more than his name, God knew him. When you attempt to encounter God, remember God knows your motives behind your intercession. He knows your strength, your weakness and the passion you have for Him. The scary thing about encountering God is that He knows everything about you; you can't hide anything from Him. The comforting thing about encountering God is that if He chooses to encounter you, He won't be surprised . . . because He already knows everything about you.

O LORD, YOU HAVE SEARCHED ME AND KNOWN ME.
YOU KNOW MY SITTING DOWN AND MY RISING UP;
YOU UNDERSTAND MY THOUGHT AFAR OFF.
PSALM 139:1,2

7. *Claim the promises of God when entering the presence of God.*
When Moses interceded to God, he reminded God that
Israel was His people and that He had promised to
bless them. Moses reminded God that He had promised to go with them into the Promised Land. Because
Moses claimed these promises by God, he was able to
get the things he asked from God.

THEN MOSES SAID TO THE LORD, "SEE, YOU SAY TO ME,
'BRING UP THIS PEOPLE.'"
EXODUS 33:12

Take-Aways
- I may have physical results from encountering God.
- I will better encounter God at certain locations.
- I will find God's name linked to His presence.
- I want to encounter God, not an angel or any other help.
- I encounter God on His terms, not mine.
- I am known by God when He comes to me.
- I must claim God's promises in His presence.

OVERCOMING FEAR*

JOHN WESLEY
FOUNDER OF METHODIST MOVEMENT, 1703-1791

In 1735 John Wesley, along with his brother Charles, journeyed to the colony of Georgia as a missionary of the Propagation Society. On the ship, John saw Moravian missionaries praying calmly in a storm while he feared for his life. This experience was influential in his later conversion to Christ. He had never appropriated Christ as his personal Savior but had been a High Anglican churchman, rigidly adhering to ritual and law with a tingling mixture of mysticism. John Wesley left Georgia a failure in his ministry to the colonists and Indians.

January 24, 1738—From the Journal of John Wesley—
I went to America, to convert the Indians; but oh, who shall convert me? who, what is he that will deliver me from this evil heart of unbelief? I have a fair summer religion. I can talk well; nay, and believe myself, while no danger is near. But let death look me in the face, and my spirit is troubled. Nor can I say, "To die is gain!"

I have a sin of fear, that when I've spun my last thread, I shall perish on the shore!

On a spring evening, John was still searching for salvation. He attended a Moravian meeting in Aldersgate where he was converted. He always looked back on this experience as his conversion.

May 14, 1738—From the Journal of John Wesley—
In the evening I went very unwillingly to a society in Aldersgate Street, where one was reading Luther's preface to the Epistle to the Romans. About a quarter before nine, while he was describing the change, which God works in the heart through faith in Christ, I felt my heart strangely warmed. I felt I did trust in Christ, Christ alone for salvation; and an assurance was given me that He had taken away my sins, even mine, and saved me from the law of sin and death.

The following spring after hearing the account of Jonathan Edwards' success in New England and of George Whitefield's successes at outdoor preaching, he began preaching in the fields. Wesley saw multitudes saved. The Methodist Revival was launched, and he remained at its head for more than 50 years. He spent the rest of his life preaching in the fields, in the streets and in the Methodist preaching chapels. He was up each morning before five o'clock for prayer and Bible study, and rode on horseback 15 to 20 miles a day, preaching four or five times daily. During his lifetime Wesley traveled 250,000 miles preaching a total of 42,000 thousand sermons. He died at the age of 88 and preached up to the very month of his death.

*   Elmer Towns, *The Christian Hall of Fame* (Grand Rapids, MI: Baker Book House, 1971), pp. 74-76.

CHAPTER 4

GIDEON:
A RELUCTANT LEADER

ENCOUNTER: OUT OF WEAK SELF-IMAGE
PLACE: UNDER AN OAK TREE
SCRIPTURE: JUDGES 6:11-24

The frail young man crawled on his hands and knees—not praying as much as he should—stooping over a pile of wheat, trying to separate wheat kernels from the husks. He was crouched in a winepress in the bottom of a ravine under a large spreading oak tree. He looked over his shoulder nervously, like a person expecting danger. He stared anxiously from bush to bush; when he was satisfied no one was spying on him, he went back to his work.

It was harvesttime in Israel, and each year roving bands of Midianites—raiders from the desert—swarmed out over the Promised Land, stealing crops just as they were harvested. Anyone who resisted was killed. Watchmen were posted on the hilltops each fall to warn the farmers when the Midianites were coming. Families quickly evacuated their farms when Midianites were reported in the area, grabbing what they could carry, running to hide in the rocks or in the woods, some even going to the mountains, not returning until the harvest was over.

Gideon looked at his large pile of wheat to be threshed and winnowed. This had been a bountiful harvest. He was grateful for God's abundance. But the sack only contained a few handfuls of grain; he still had a lot of work to do. It would take all winter to finish the task.

Gideon rose from his hands and knees to stretch his aching back. Closing his eyes, he thought of the past when he was a young boy. He remembered how the family worked together to winnow the wheat, going to the tallest hill on their farm. He would beat the wheat with a stick to separate the kernels from their shells. The family worked as a unit in the late afternoon, the time of day when a brisk wind blew across the hilltop. The wind was necessary to winnow the grain. His father took a shovel to toss the heads of crushed wheat into the air, and the wind blew the chaff away. The kernels fell into a blanket. Then his sisters swept any stray kernels into sacks. It took only two or three days to winnow the grain for the bread they ate for the rest of the year.

But Gideon was hiding down in a low, cool spot where they pressed out olives and grapes. He could winnow only one handful at a time. He'd roll a round stone over the wheat to separate the kernels from the shell, one handful at a time. He'd blow the chaff away, one handful at a time. He'd pour grain into his sack, one handful at a time.

Gideon jumped back into the hole to work, crawling around the winepress on his hands and knees. Each puff of breath produced a small handful of grain. Each puff of breath produced enough flour for bread for one day for one person in his family. He knew it would take all winter to winnow the wheat. Then suddenly Gideon's thoughts were interrupted.

"Greetings," a voice called to him. There, sitting on a rock a few steps away, was a stranger who didn't look Jewish, nor did he appear to be a Midianite; the stranger was different.

Gideon flinched and then jumped to his feet. He was scared but didn't have a weapon. He was not sure if he could use a weapon if one were available.

"Greetings," the stranger spoke again. "You are God's hero. You are courageous."

Gideon thought the greeting was absurd. The stranger was complimenting him for his courage but he was afraid of everyone, even the one talking to him. *This stranger doesn't understand that the Midianites invade our land every fall,* Gideon thought. *This fellow must be from some foreign country.* Then Gideon blurted out in response to the absurd greetings, "If I am a hero of God,"—Gideon was young, so he wanted to be respectful—"if I have courage, why am I hiding in this ravine from the Midianites? Why am I groveling on my hands and knees for a few kernels of grain?"

The stranger was not a warrior from the Midianites, nor was he from any other country. The stranger had a message to Gideon from God. The stranger explained, "The Lord is with you." He waited to see Gideon's response before continuing. "You will be courageous because the Lord will be with you."

The stranger explained to Gideon that he was not a strong man in himself, but that he could be strong in his God. Even though he was hiding under an oak tree, God would make him courageous. But Gideon wasn't sure. He answered, "If God is with me,"—the scared Gideon halted his speech—"if God is with us, where are the miracles He can do?" Gideon had seen families killed, so where was God? Gideon had heard the elders in the village beaten, so where was God? Gideon had seen his father's crops stolen, so where was God? God had not answered his prayers.

"If God is with His people," Gideon asked, "why doesn't He do miracles for us like He did when He brought Israel out of Egypt?" The depressed Gideon was not being disrespectful, nor did he have a bitter heart. But it's hard to believe that the water is hot if you can't see steam rising from the pot. Gideon believed in God and wanted God to protect Israel, but the suffering of God's people perplexed him. "God has forsaken us," Gideon went on. "He has delivered us into the hands of the Midianites. We can't do anything about our suffering; God is punishing us."

The stranger, still sitting on the rock, explained to Gideon that God had heard the prayers of families from all over the nation. God knew Israel was sorry for her sin. God heard Israel crying out for deliverance. Then the stranger told Gideon, "God will use you to deliver Israel from the Midianites. You will be courageous in the strength of the Lord. You will fight in the strength of the Lord. You will drive the Midianites away in God's power."

"Not me!" Gideon exclaimed without thinking. "I can't deliver Israel from the Midianites. They are too strong; there are too many . . ."

The idea of leading an army into battle was beyond young Gideon's imagination. He was not a powerful general like Joshua, nor was he a mighty warrior like Caleb. Gideon had a low self-image. Lacking self-confidence he said, "I am the youngest in my father's family . . . my father is the poorest in the Abiezrite clan . . . our clan is the smallest in the tribe of Manasseh . . . and Manasseh is the weakest of the 12 tribes of Israel."

The stranger listened to Gideon's excuses and then spoke to build up the young man's confidence. "I will be with you; and with My power, you will defeat the Midianites."

Gideon had asked the stranger why God was not with Israel to defeat the Midianites. Now the stranger was claiming He would be with Gideon to defeat them. Gideon wondered, *Is this stranger claiming to be God?* He decided to put the stranger to a test. "If I have found grace in Your sight, then show me a miracle to prove that You will use me to destroy the Midianites."

Remembering that his family always brought a sacrifice when they went to Shiloh to worship God at the Tabernacle, Gideon decided that if the stranger was truly God, he should bring a blood sacrifice to Him, just as his father brought a lamb to the priest to sacrifice for sin. So Gideon put together a plan. "Will you wait while I run to the house and prepare an offering for You?" he asked.

The stranger responded, "I will wait here for you."

Gideon sprang into action. He ran quickly up the ravine toward the family home, toward the pen where the young lambs were kept. Gideon selected a small lamb, perfect and unblemished. He sacrificed it just the way he had seen others do. Carefully, Gideon placed pieces of flesh from the slain lamb into a basket. He planned to carry the pieces of lamb back to the winepress hidden in a basket, so no one would know what he was doing.

Then Gideon remembered that at the annual Passover feast, unleavened bread was brought to God. Gideon scooped a whole pot of flour from the sack in the family storeroom. He wanted to have enough flour to make a big offering to God.

As Gideon returned to the oak tree, he wondered if the stranger would still be there. Would He wait on someone as insignificant as the youngest son in the poorest family of the area?

The stranger was still sitting on the rock, waiting. Gideon bowed his head and bent his shoulders in homage. Holding his offerings with outstretched arms, Gideon slowly approached the rock and the stranger. He did not attempt to make eye contact.

Gideon placed the basket and pot at the bottom of the large rock, and in the same motion, nodded to the stranger that the presents were for Him. Gideon presented his gifts as carefully as he had seen his father offer sacrifices to God. He wanted to do everything right.

The stranger stepped off the rock and then nodded his head in approval—both approval of Gideon and his offerings—then motioned to the top of the rock. "Take the young lamb and take the unleavened bread and spread them on top of this large smooth rock."

Gideon obeyed. He spread strips of flesh on the rock, arranging the pieces just as he had seen his father, his grandfather and the other men of the village do. Next, Gideon spread the unleavened bread on the rock.

Suddenly Gideon realized something was missing. There was no wood on the large rock. Gideon was worried, but then the stranger stepped toward the rock, stopped momentarily and reached out his staff, touching the meat and the unleavened bread in a gesture of acceptance. And then the miracle Gideon had hoped for happened right before his eyes, as the rock burst into flames, consuming the flesh and the unleavened bread.

Being a thinker—not a doer—Gideon wondered what this miracle meant. He remembered that the stranger had told him that he was to lead Israel to defeat the Midianites. *Would he become a soldier? And who was this stranger? Was He a miracle worker like Moses? Was He an angel of the Lord? Could He be a form of God?*

Then, without warning, Gideon got his answer. The stranger didn't tell him what He would do, nor did the stranger say anything else to Gideon. The stranger simply disappeared into heaven in the smoke of the offering.

"Oh God!" Gideon cried with a loud voice. He now knew he had seen God—or at least the Angel of the Lord—face-to-face. The

Jewish scribes didn't know who the Angel of the Lord was, but they knew when someone saw Him that it was the same as seeing God, and they knew the Angel of the Lord had claimed to be God.

Underneath the giant oak, Gideon raised his clenched fist to heaven and, shaking with fear, cried out, "I have seen God face-to-face, and I shall die." Still the pessimist, Gideon expected the worst from God. He expected to be punished, not blessed by Him.

The last of the smoke drifted between the oak branches, and a few hot coals were cooling. Gideon stood in the reflection of a miracle and shook with fear. Then he heard God speak from heaven. "Gideon, you shall not die. Peace. I have made peace with you because of this sacrificial offering."

AFTER THE ENCOUNTER

Gideon was used of God to drive the Midianites out of Israel, but even before doing that, Gideon continued to have self-doubts and lack of confidence in God's Word. He wouldn't destroy his father's grove of trees in the daytime where Baal was worshipped; he did it by night when no one was looking. He sought further confirmation from God by putting out a fleece of wool and asking God to make it wet over night. When God did it, Gideon asked for the opposite the next night. He was never sure of God's plan, but he eventually obeyed. Three hundred men took pitchers, trumpets and torches to confuse the enemy, who then slaughtered themselves. Gideon was God's leader to drive the enemy from his homeland.

What Gideon Learned in Meeting God

1. *Oppression from circumstances or by an enemy is God's response to His people's rebellion.* God always wants to give the best things to His children, but many times they refuse

to live by His principles that will bring them His blessings. When they rebel, God allows them to suffer the consequences of their sin. Sin is the root cause for the problems of God's people.

SO THE PEOPLE SERVED THE LORD ALL THE DAYS OF JOSHUA, AND ALL THE DAYS OF THE ELDERS WHO OUTLIVED JOSHUA. ANOTHER GENERATION AROSE AFTER THEM WHO DID NOT KNOW THE LORD NOR THE WORK WHICH HE HAD DONE FOR ISRAEL. THEN THE CHILDREN OF ISRAEL DID EVIL IN THE SIGHT OF THE LORD, AND SERVED THE BAALS. AND THE ANGER OF THE LORD WAS HOT AGAINST ISRAEL. SO HE DELIVERED THEM INTO THE HANDS OF PLUNDERERS.

JUDGES 2:7,10,11,14

2. *When God's people cry out for deliverance, God calls someone to deliver them.* God sent the Midianites to punish Israel for their sin. "Then the children of Israel did evil in the sight of the LORD. So the LORD delivered them into the hand of Midian for seven years" (Judg. 6:1). God lets His people suffer the consequences of their rebellion until they cry for relief. "[T]he children of Israel cried out to the LORD because of the Midianites" (v. 7). God's deliverance comes through His servant; He must find a faithful person, encounter him or her with the task and send him or her to do it.

NEVERTHELESS, THE LORD RAISED UP JUDGES WHO DELIVERED THEM OUT OF THE HAND OF THOSE WHO PLUNDERED THEM.

JUDGES 2:16

3. *God usually encounters those who are faithfully working, even though their task may seem small and their results seem to make little contribution.* Gideon was a coward, hiding among the trees to winnow a little flour. While Gideon's task was pathetic, at least he was faithfully working at something. God saw a small spark in Gideon and used him for a great victory.

NOT MANY MIGHTY, NOT MANY NOBLE, ARE CALLED. BUT GOD HAS CHOSEN THE FOOLISH THINGS OF THE WORLD TO PUT TO SHAME THE WISE, AND GOD HAS CHOSEN THE WEAK THINGS OF THE WORLD TO PUT TO SHAME THE THINGS WHICH ARE MIGHTY.

I CORINTHIANS 1:26,27

4. *The Lord encounters people at their level of unbelief or negative self-image.* Gideon had a poor self-image and had trouble trusting God. He was not a courageous leader nor did he lead from boldness. God confronted Gideon's emotional problems when He encountered him to prepare Gideon for service. We can learn from Gideon's encounter with God that He will stretch us to a larger task than we can do in our own strength because He will be with us to get it done.

THEN THE DISCIPLES CAME TO JESUS PRIVATELY AND SAID, "WHY COULD WE NOT CAST IT OUT?" SO JESUS SAID TO THEM, "BECAUSE OF YOUR UNBELIEF; . . . IF YOU HAVE FAITH AS A MUSTARD SEED, . . . NOTHING WILL BE IMPOSSIBLE FOR YOU."

MATTHEW 17:19,20

5. *God patiently waits for some people because He understands their weakness.* When Gideon wanted to give God a present, he left the Lord and ran to prepare a sacrifice. God patiently waited while Gideon brought the sacrifice and presented it to Him. On other occasions, God makes the recipient wait, such as Paul who prayed and fasted three days. Also, God cleansed Isaiah with coals from off the altar, but on this occasion, God waited for Gideon.

OUT OF THE MOUTH OF BABES . . . YOU HAVE ORDAINED
STRENGTH, BECAUSE OF YOUR ENEMIES, THAT YOU MAY
SILENCE THE ENEMY AND THE AVENGER.
PSALM 8:2

6. *What a person gets from an encounter with God becomes characteristic of that person's remembrance of that experience.* Gideon thought he would die because of encountering God. God told him, "You will not die." In that response Gideon learned he had made peace with God. In today's terminology, people say they have "made peace with their soul," which is one expression of salvation. Gideon built a permanent altar at the spot where he encountered God, calling it "Jehovah-shalom," which means "the Lord is peace" (see Judg. 6:24). Gideon remembered making peace with God at that spot when he encountered God.

SO GIDEON BUILT AN ALTAR THERE TO THE LORD, AND
CALLED IT THE-LORD-IS-PEACE. TO THIS DAY IT IS STILL IN
OPHRAH OF THE ABIEZRITES.
JUDGES 6:24

7. *Sometimes the place we encounter God becomes reverent and remembered.* Gideon called the place the "oak of Ophrah," and the altar was called "Jehovah-Shalom." Then the writer adds, "To this day it is yet in Ophrah of the Abiezrites."

A few have erected chapels or churches over places where they encountered God. Others remember an altar at a camp meeting or a place at a church or in a bedroom where they knelt to surrender their lives to God. Some like to return to a specific spot to renew their vows to God. Whether we revisit the spot in our mind or actually return to the physical location, the important thing to remember is that there actually was a time and place we met God, and we can meet God again . . . anytime . . . anyplace . . . any day.

BUT YOU SHALL SEEK THE PLACE WHERE THE LORD YOUR GOD CHOOSES, OUT OF ALL YOUR TRIBES, TO PUT HIS NAME FOR HIS DWELLING PLACE; AND THERE YOU SHALL GO.
DEUTERONOMY 12:5

Take-Aways

- I will eventually seek God when oppressed.
- I can be delivered from fear by encountering God.
- I will be encountered by God if I am faithful.
- I don't have to overcome all unbelief for God's encounter.
- God waits patiently because He understands our weaknesses.
- I will be permanently influenced by an encounter with God.
- I remember the place God encountered me.

A NEW MORNING

JOE FOCHT
PASTOR, CALVARY CHAPEL
PHILADELPHIA, PENNSYLVANIA

I was playing guitar in a rock band traveling throughout the East Coast in the early '80s. I was dropping acid, smoking pot and living like most of the youth who were characterized as "hippies." I was deeply into Eastern mysticism when a good friend witnessed to me about Christ, asking me to be converted. I didn't understand what my friend meant. Occasionally I picked up a Bible and read it, but Eastern mysticism had gripped me. I was searching for God. I would drop LSD, sit in front of an open window in the winter time without a shirt, breathe deeply and read my Bible.

I saw what I thought was a loophole in Christianity; I saw a difference between Jesus as a Savior and Jesus as a Teacher. But I still sought reality in the Eastern religions. I'd put a blanket over my head and go into deep meditation. I went to see the Maharaja who was on a whirlwind tour of the United States. The Maharaja was nothing but a fat little kid from India that "blew in my ear." He was supposed to be blowing meditative thoughts in my ear about God.

I was playing a gig in the Pocono Mountains at Skinner's Fall, Pennsylvania, when Harris Gordon, a friend, talked with me about Christ until 3:00 A.M. one morning. He asked me to pray. The presence of the Lord fell upon the room, and we both wept unashamedly before the Lord. I experienced the personage of the Holy Spirit in the room. Jesus was not visible, but I knew He was there. I hung my head and cried, feeling ashamed for all my sins. I repented of all my sins. I felt wave upon wave of God's grace washing upon me. That night I got my soul right before God, was forgiven of my sins, and Christ came into my life.

The next morning I saw the sky bluer than ever before; my total life was absolutely transformed. Some friends called and asked me to come to a pentecostal church and pray at the altar to receive Christ, but I told them it had already happened in my life.*

---

* Joe Focht later began Calvary Chapel in Philadelphia, Pennsylvania, in a catering hall, and 17 years later the church was the largest in Northeast United States, with over 10,000 children and adults in attendance weekly.

CHAPTER 5

ELIJAH:
HEARING GOD'S SMALL VOICE

ENCOUNTERING: OUT OF DISCOURAGEMENT
PLACE: IN A CAVE ON SINAI
SCRIPTURE: 1 KINGS 19:1-18

The dull gray Negev desert stretched flat in every direction, its only beauty in the fine crystal sand and various rock formations that splash their way up from the sea of sand.

A lone traveler stumbled down the road, heading south away from the Promised Land. The stranger—without a water bottle—staggered into the teeth of the desert as though he were seeking a miserable way to commit suicide.

Beersheba was the southernmost oasis in the Holy Land, the last drink of water before launching out into the desert. No one ventured south on the highway alone—without water—no one in his right mind.

But Elijah was God's unpredictable prophet; he never did what people expected. He was God's champion. The previous week he unexpectedly faced 400 priests of the false god Baal on top of Mount Carmel. It was a showdown of power. The false priest prayed for fire from heaven, but nothing came. Then Elijah did the unexpected. He poured water over the wood and sacrifice—three times. Then he knelt before Jehovah, the God of Israel, to ask for fire to be poured out from heaven like water from a bucket. Bold Elijah was vindicated when God sent the fire. He immediately turned and pointed to the 400 false prophets and yelled to the crowd, "Kill them!"

But victory was short-lived. When Queen Jezebel heard that Elijah had killed her prophets, she sent a royal decree to Elijah by messenger: "I will kill you by this hour tomorrow!"

That's when Elijah ran away. He could stand against 400 false prophets of Baal—he was bold—but a woman sent him running. He ran almost 100 miles, evading the queen's soldiers, bypassing every village and town, avoiding people and living off the land, sleeping in caves, until finally escaping to Beersheba.

"They won't look for me in the desert," he said to himself as he launched out over the sandy wastelands. Then he saw it, among the rising heat vapors on the horizon, like a hallucination that fades then reappears: a lone juniper tree, one day's journey south of the oasis, the shade he needed to survive. But instead of enjoying the cool relief from the blistering sun, he realized the futility of his situation. If he returned to the Holy Land, he'd die. If he went into the desert, he'd die. In utter frustration, Elijah looked to heaven and prayed, "Kill me, God. I don't deserve to live."

Perspiration dampened his tunic, he became dizzy, and he passed out into sleep. He slept fitfully in the hot, late-afternoon sun. Hours later, the cool night desert air chilled him. He had gone from heat exhaustion to bone-shaking chills. He pulled his robe tight for comfort. He was trying to sleep when he felt something—or someone—poking him.

He jerked himself awake. "Who's there?"

"I'm an angel from God."

Sitting up, Elijah looked around. He saw red coals glowing in a campfire, smelled the unmistakable aroma of baked cake. There was a water bottle, full of crystal-clear water, waiting for him.

"Get up," the angel instructed him. "Eat and drink; you have a long journey before you."

Elijah drank first because his bodily fluids were depleted. With every swallow, he could feel life surging through his parched body. Then, tearing at the cake, Elijah shoveled huge chunks into his mouth. It didn't bother him that he swallowed sand from his beard with the cake and water. He no longer wanted to die; he was glad to be alive, even though his situation was precarious. Within minutes, Elijah was full and he was sound asleep once again.

Elijah hovered under the shade of the juniper all the next day, sick from overeating and from the heat. That night the cold desert wind again chilled his sleep. He tried to find protection behind a sand dune. Again, the angel had to poke Elijah two or three times to awaken him. Coming out of a deep sleep, Elijah could barely discern the words, "Rise and eat." The angel had prepared another meal.

"Eat plenty and drink well," the angel instructed him. "You have 40 days of fasting ahead of you, as it will take you that long to get to your destination."

Elijah immediately knew the destination; there was only one place south of Beersheba where God would send someone. "Horeb," Elijah whispered. "The mountain of God."

"Now sleep," the angel instructed him. "The journey is great; you'll need all your strength."

40 Days Later

Elijah stood at the bottom of Sinai, the tallest mountain in the Horeb range. Looking almost straight up, he knew God had met

Moses at the top, so he had to go up there, too. *If I want to see God,* Elijah thought, *I'll have to go to the top.*

Slowly and painstakingly, Elijah followed the steep, treacherous path. As Elijah passed the tree line, the weather cooled. Toward evening, Elijah saw a large cave, protected from the cold evening wind. He slept in the cave that evening. The next morning God spoke to him. "Elijah, what are you doing here at Sinai?"

At first Elijah didn't know how to answer the question. God had provided food and water to save him in the desert. God had led him to Sinai. Now God was asking why he was here. He responded, "I've been very jealous for Your glory, oh, Lord God of Israel. Israel has rejected her covenant with You, destroyed Your altars and killed Your prophets."

Discouragement was evident in Elijah's voice. He raged against the sin of God's people and then concluded with finality, "I'm the only one left who is true to You. I've run away because they tried to kill me."

God didn't want to hear excuses, nor was He interested in giving pity to Elijah. God had some things to show Elijah. "Go stand on the top of Sinai," God instructed him.

On the peak of Sinai, Elijah could look down in every direction. He was higher than he'd ever been in his life, and he felt closer to God than he'd ever been. He could feel God's presence, even as he had a couple of months earlier on Mount Carmel where fire whooshed down from heaven.

Suddenly a storm began forming off to the right. It was a snarling black cloud, a rain cloud, a hurricane. The storm began moving toward Elijah and passed right in front of him. The gray early morning turned dark—black like midnight. A powerful wind and rushing clouds swept before him, faster than any rushing storm he'd ever seen, faster than any wind he'd ever experienced.

But the wind didn't touch Elijah; he saw it but didn't feel it. The wind gushed over the rocks before him, dislodging even the largest of boulders and sending them plunging down the cliff, splitting as they plunged over other rocks. The sound of smashing rocks and howling winds was deafening. Suddenly the wind ceased and the clouds were gone. Then Elijah experienced silence.

Elijah didn't see the Lord in the wind. He knew God was there, but he couldn't see Him.

Then the earth began to quake, but Elijah wasn't afraid. The top of the mountain shook like never before, and no one was there to see it except God and Elijah. Great crevices opened in the side of the mountain, and more rocks began tumbling down the steep slopes of Sinai. The earthquake stopped just as suddenly as it started. Then Elijah experienced silence.

Elijah didn't see the Lord in the earthquake, but he still knew God was there.

Then off to the left, Elijah saw fire, like the fire of the *Shekinah* Glory Cloud but brighter. The fire roared with a burning noise, flames dancing in the sky. Then, suddenly, it disappeared. Elijah again felt silence.

Elijah didn't see God in the wind, in the earthquake, in the fire. He wondered, *Where is God?*

Off in the distance he heard it. Turning his ear to the right, he strained to hear, but the breeze, made it difficult. Elijah turned and retreated down on the path, trying to get away from the breeze, so he could hear the sound clearly. All was still and quiet in the mouth of the cave. Cupping his hand to his ear, he listened intently.

Elijah heard a still, small voice.

God was not shouting, nor did God demand attention. The Lord whispered, "What are you doing here at Sinai?"

This was the second time God had asked Elijah this question. Elijah wasn't sure why God was asking him that question, so he gave the same answer he'd given the first time: "I have been very jealous of Your presence, oh, Lord God of Israel. Israel has rejected Your covenant, destroyed Your altars and killed Your prophets. I am the only one left who is faithful to You." Then he added, "They seek my life to kill me!"

God knew that sympathy was not what the discouraged prophet needed. He had a task for Elijah. "Go to the capital city of Damascus and anoint Hazael king over Syria."

Surely this task was a death sentence to Israel; Hazael would try to destroy God's people. But God wasn't finished. He had other terrifying news for Elijah. "Go to Israel and anoint Jehu king over Israel."

Jehu was a general in the army of God's people, with a reputation of being unrelenting, demanding and vicious in battle. Also, Jehu would murder anyone who tried to take his kingdom.

God still had other tasks for Elijah. "Go anoint the young prophet Elisha to take your place."

Then God explained the purpose of Elijah's assigned tasks. "Those that escape the sword of Hazael will be killed by the sword of Jehu. Those that escape the sword of Jehu will be slain by the sword of Elisha the prophet."

Storm clouds were gathering on the horizon, and destruction was coming. To further equip Elijah for the difficulties he would face, God corrected His earlier statement by saying, "There are 7,000 persons in Israel who have not bowed their knee to Baal, 7,000 persons who worship Jehovah and serve Me."

AFTER THE ENCOUNTER

Elijah sent the prophet Elisha to anoint Hazael, who was much more vicious toward God's people than his predecessor (see

2 Kings 8:12); then another prophet anointed Jehu, again a king more vicious than his predecessor. Finally, Elijah anointed Elisha in his place. But Elijah had some time and ministry left. Before Elijah was taken to heaven, he did other miracles and influenced the kingdom in other ways.

Elijah's Lessons in Running into God

1. *God will encounter those who are running from Him.* When Jezebel threatened to kill Elijah, he began running for his life, crossing through Israel and Judea, then venturing out into the desert. He ended up at Mount Sinai where God encountered him, sending him back into ministry.

GO, RETURN ON YOUR WAY.

I KINGS 19:15

2. *God asks questions when He encounters us, not because He wants information, but to teach us something.* Notice in the Scriptures how God came to Adam asking, "Adam, where are you?" And then God asked Cain, "Why are you angry?" When God encountered Elijah he asked, "What are you doing here, Elijah?" God did not ask the question to get information; God knows all things. God wanted Elijah to face his conscience and motivations. Elijah had run away from the people to whom God had called him to minister. He was running for the wrong reasons. God asked a question to make Elijah honestly face his unbelief.

SEARCH ME, O GOD, AND KNOW MY HEART;
TRY ME, AND KNOW MY ANXIETIES; AND SEE IF THERE IS
ANY WICKED WAY IN ME, AND LEAD ME
IN THE WAY EVERLASTING.
PSALM 139:23,24

3. *Sometimes a physical fast from food is associated with an encounter with God.* Although there are times when we may need to take care of our physical needs before meeting with God, as in the case of the angel ministering to Elijah's need for food and water, there are other times when a fast can accompany an encounter with God. Some people meet God and then begin fasting, as Saul fasted for three days after seeing Jesus on the Damascus road. In this case, Elijah fasted for 40 days before he encountered God on Mount Sinai.

Fasting is a time when you refrain from food so that you give all your attention to seeking God. You abstain from food, but hunger and thirst after righteousness, seeking a spiritual answer from God. Sometimes prayer is not enough. You take your intercession to a higher level through fasting.

This could have been a forced fast, since Elijah may not have had food available between the juniper tree and Mount Sinai. Whatever the case, he fasted before he encountered God.

IS NOT THIS THE FAST THAT I HAVE CHOSEN?
. . . THAT YE BREAK EVERY YOKE?
ISAIAH 58:6, *KJV*

4. *Sometimes we won't like what we hear when God encounters us.* Elijah had run away from Queen Jezebel, fearing for his life. But God encountered him and sent him back to his homeland with a threefold task. He was to anoint Hazael king of Syria, Jehu king of Israel, Elisha as a prophet to replace him. The kings that Elijah anointed were vicious men and anointing them was probably a task that Elijah didn't want to do. Also, when he anointed Elisha to take his place, he had to deal with his own humanity and frailty. No one likes to step aside to allow someone else to take his place. Yet Elijah encountered God, and from that experience he received enough strength to do tasks that were unpleasant.

IF MY PEOPLE WHO ARE CALLED BY MY NAME
WILL HUMBLE THEMSELVES, AND PRAY
AND SEEK MY FACE, AND TURN FROM THEIR WICKED WAYS,
THEN I WILL HEAR FROM HEAVEN, AND WILL FORGIVE
THEIR SIN AND HEAL THEIR LAND.
2 CHRONICLES 7:14

5. *Action is the best thing to break discouragement or emotional collapse.* Often we try to get discouraged people to rationalize why they are discouraged. We try to deal with an emotional problem by academic means, but that doesn't always work. The best way to get the attention of those struggling with an emotional problem is to put them to work. God gave the discouraged Elijah a task—but not just any task. The task involved

the future. Many people are discouraged because they have no future—no hope. Elijah needed to look beyond the present kings of Israel. Surely King Ahab and Queen Jezebel wanted to kill him, but God told him to anoint Jehu in their place, i.e., look to the future. The greatest enemy that God's people had at the time was the king of Syria, and God told Elijah to anoint the next king of that nation. Then God wanted him to look beyond his own life, so God told him to anoint Elisha. In this way, God was assuring Elijah that His work would continue after Elijah's death.

WHATEVER [JESUS] SAYS TO YOU, DO IT.
JOHN 2:5

6. *When you encounter someone who lowers his or her voice, you must become still and quiet if you want to hear and understand him or her.* God did not just use miracles to speak to Elijah, nor did He speak to him in the wind or the fire. God lowered His voice to get Elijah's full attention. Sometimes we must be still and listen if we want to encounter God.

BE STILL, AND KNOW THAT I AM GOD.
PSALM 46:10

7. *You can get hope and encouragement in an encounter with God.* Elijah had been used greatly of God; there was an

anointing for service upon his life. For three and a half years at the brook Cherith, God used ravens to supernaturally provide food for Elijah. Then Elijah went to the town of Zarephath where God miraculously provided for his needs by using a widow with a cruse of oil and a barrel of meal that did not run out during a famine. Then, when the widow's son died, Elijah raised him from the dead. There was the famous confrontation with the prophets of Baal on Mount Carmel. Elijah prayed and God sent fire from heaven. In spite of all that God did for him, Elijah got discouraged. This means that perhaps you have been used of God in the past but now you too are discouraged. Like Elijah, God can break your discouragement by encountering you for future ministry.

YET I HAVE RESERVED SEVEN THOUSAND IN ISRAEL, ALL WHOSE KNEES HAVE NOT BOWED TO BAAL, AND EVERY MOUTH THAT HAS NOT KISSED HIM.

I KINGS 19:18

Take-Aways

- I may be encountered by God even when I run from Him.
- I must answer questions about my motivation.
- I can fast to prepare for an encounter.
- I won't always like what I hear in an encounter.
- I can break discouragement with action.
- I will pay better attention when God lowers His voice.
- I will return to service after an encounter with God.

AWAKENED ZEAL*

OSWALD CHAMBERS
AUTHOR, *MY UTMOST FOR HIS HIGHEST*

I was in Dunoon College as a tutor in philosophy when Dr. F. B. Meyer came and spoke about the Holy Spirit. I determined to have all that was going, and went to my room and asked God simply and definitely for the baptism of the Holy Spirit, whatever that meant.

God used me during those years for the conversion of souls, but I had no conscious communion with Him. The Bible was the

dullest, most uninteresting book in existence, and the vileness
and bad-motiveness of my nature was terrific.

The last three months of those years things reached a climax,
I was getting very desperate. I knew no one who had what I wanted; in fact I did not know what I did want. But I knew that if what
I had was all the Christianity there was, the thing was a fraud.
Then Luke 11:13 got hold of me—"If ye then, being evil, know
how to give good gifts to your children. How much more shall
your heavenly Father give the Holy Spirit to them that ask Him?"

But how could I, bad motivated as I was, possibly ask for the
gift of the Holy Spirit? Then it was borne in upon me that I had
to claim the gift from God on the authority of Jesus Christ and
testify to having done so. But the thought came—if you claim
the gift of the Holy Spirit on the Word of Jesus Christ and testify to it, God will make it known to those who know you best how
bad you are in heart. God brings one to the point of utter
despair, and I got to the place where I did not care whether
everyone knew how bad I was; I cared for nothing on earth, sav-
ing to get out of my present condition.

At a little meeting held during a mission in Dunoon, a well-
known lady was asked to take the afternoon meeting. She did
not speak, but set us to prayer, and then sang "Touch me again,
Lord." I felt nothing, but I knew emphatically my time had
come, and I rose to my feet. I had no vision of God, only a sheer
dogged determination to take God at His Word and to prove
this thing for myself, and I stood up and said so.

That was bad enough, but what followed was ten times
worse. After I had sat down the lady worker, who knew me well,
said: "That is very good of our brother, he has spoken like that
as an example to the rest of you."

Up I got again and said: "I got up for no one (else's) sake, I
got up for my own sake; either Christianity is a downright fraud,

or I have not got hold of the right end of the stick." And then and there I claimed the gift of the Holy Spirit in dogged commitment on Luke 11:13.

I had no vision of heaven or of angels, I had nothing. I was as dry and empty as ever, no power or realization of God, no witness of the Holy Spirit. Then I was asked to speak at a meeting, and 40 souls came out to the front. Did I praise God? No, I was terrified and left them to the workers, and went to Mr. MacGregor (a friend) and told him what had happened, and he said: "Don't you remember claiming the Holy Spirit as a gift on the word of Jesus, and that He said: 'Ye shall receive power . . . ?' This is the power from on high." Then like a flash something happened inside me, and I saw that I had been wanting power in my own hand, so to speak, that I might say—Look what I have by putting my all on the altar.

If the four previous years had been hell on earth, these five years have truly been heaven on earth. Glory be to God, the last aching abyss of the human heart is filled to overflowing with the love of God. Love is the beginning, love is the middle and love is the end. After He comes in, all you see is "Jesus only, Jesus ever."

* V. Raymond Edman, *They Found the Secret* (Grand Rapids, MI: Zondervan Publishing House, 1984), pp. 33, 34.

CHAPTER 6

ISAIAH:
PROPHET FOR GOD

ENCOUNTER: WHEN DREAMS ARE DESTROYED
PLACE: IN THE TEMPLE IN JERUSALEM
SCRIPTURE: ISAIAH 6:1-13

The king's funeral had lasted longer than everyone expected, the crowd was much larger then anticipated, and there were more speakers than usual. But the most shocking event of all was that King Uzziah was buried among the kings of Judah.

After the funeral was over, Isaiah, a young member of Uzziah's court, waited at Uzziah's tomb longer than anyone else from the official funeral delegation. Young Isaiah loved old Uzziah and believed in the king's dreams. He had believed Uzziah could restore the glory of David to Jerusalem. Now the king was dead, and Isaiah's dreams were gone, but an ugly fight had broken out over his burial place. Some didn't want King Uzziah's vault to be located near the burial place of David and Solomon. One rabbi had argued, "Uzziah sinned."

The rabbis had announced to the great Sanhedrin—a meeting where religious matters were settled—"Because Uzziah sinned, he disgraced the office of king. He shall not be buried with the great kings . . . with David and Solomon."

Uzziah had been a great king—greater than any king they'd had in quite some time, having served for 52 years. Uzziah captured territory that the Philistines had stolen from Judah; he built fortresses and a harbor city on the gulf of Aquaba, and strengthened the walls of Jerusalem. Another rabbi defended the burial of Uzziah. "Uzziah made the walls of Jerusalem stronger . . . higher . . . and he invented new weapons to protect us. We are a stronger nation because of Uzziah."

The entire Sanhedrin agreed that Jerusalem was more secure from attack than before. Under Uzziah, the army had invented a catapult to hurl huge rocks at the enemy. The army had also invented a machine to shoot multiple arms, raining mass destruction on an attacking enemy. The defender of Uzziah who wanted him buried with the great kings argued, "Uzziah has given us more security . . . more prosperity . . . more prestige . . . than any other king."

Yes, Uzziah had reigned well for 52 years, but one last arrogant act overshadowed the memory of his accomplishments. In defiance against God, Uzziah walked into the holy Temple where only God's priests could go. He brought a lamb to sacrifice, a task only God's priests could carry out. Uzziah also took the golden censer into the holy place to offer prayers to God, a duty only priests could perform.

"Treason!" a young priest yelled at King Uzziah. He dashed off to get the Temple guard, yelling to all as he ran, "The King is mad! The King is mad! The King is mad!" The young priest soon returned with the high priest, the inner council and over 50 temple guards and 400 priests, all of whom surrounded the king.

The confrontation exploded at the table of incense in the holy place.

"Uzziah, you have sinned against God," shouted the high priest, trying to grab the golden censer from the king.

"How dare you stop me!" Uzziah yelled back, clutching the censer to his chest.

Uzziah's success had gone to his head; he had forgotten that God had separated the office of king and priest. No one could cross that line—not even a successful king. Their offices were determined by birth, the kings coming from the line of Judah, the priests from the line of Levi.

As the high priest attempted to yank the golden censer from the king, his mouth dropped open in amazement and terror. A large patch of white leprosy had broken out on the king's forehead, its red infection streaking down onto the rest of his face. The high priest jumped back in horror, screaming the warning, "Leprosy!"

The jostling crowd of priests, guards and the king's entourage froze in fear. God had commanded that no leper could enter the Temple; yet here in the holy place, God had stricken Uzziah with leprosy. Everyone knew the disease was a sign of inner secret sin and meant certain premature death. Uzziah's inner rebellion was now evidenced on his face.

"Unclean!" yelled the young priest who had first encountered Uzziah in the Temple. "Unclean! Unclean!"

Uzziah resigned his office as king, and his son Jotham took his place. Uzziah lived the rest of his short life in a house separated from society, as prescribed by the law.

Yet, in spite of his last act of rebellion, Uzziah was buried in the vaults along with the great kings of Judah, only a few feet from King David and King Solomon. Now the funeral was over, and the dreams of Uzziah were gone. Because of his emotional attachment to the late king, Isaiah felt the nation couldn't go on without Uzziah. His world was collapsing around him, and yet he had not given up hope. Even until the last he had prayed, "God, heal King Uzziah," but God hadn't answered. Now Isaiah stood before the burial crypt thinking, *Our nation was so close to returning to the glory of David. So close . . . we almost made it.*

Every Jew had a dream of living in the kingdom of David, feeling the security of David's protection, enjoying the prosperity of David. Isaiah thought Uzziah could have returned the past glory to Judah. King Jotham was not as strong as his father and not as wise or as godly. Isaiah prayed to God, "What will happen to us now?" Finally, in desperation, Isaiah left the tomb and walked toward the Temple, thinking, "Perhaps in God's presence I can understand."

Isaiah was recognized in the city as a bright, young, rising leader, though somewhat arrogant. The old leaders knew Isaiah had a keen mind and that he was articulate, and they expected him to sit on the great Sanhedrin one day. But they also knew Isaiah had a strong ego.

As Isaiah walked through the Golden Gate into the Temple, the priests nodded, but Isaiah was too haughty to return their greetings. Mysteriously drawn to the place where his dreams were destroyed, he looked to heaven through tear-blurred eyes and cried out, "Why?" Then Isaiah beheld what he had never seen before. The skies opened and clouds were folded back as Isaiah was allowed to look into heaven.

And then Isaiah saw the Lord sitting on the throne. He saw a rainbow around the throne, with flashes of lightning coming from its midst. But Isaiah didn't focus on the throne or the things around it; he focused only on the One sitting upon it.

"I see the Lord," he said quietly, awestruck at the magnificence of his vision. "I see the Lord, sitting high upon a throne in heaven." Immediately, Isaiah fell on his knees with his face to the ground. Then he heard the sound of wings fluttering, like hundreds of pigeons flapping their wings against the air to lift themselves into the sky. Looking up, he saw angels and heard them singing praises to God. He joined them in singing, "Holy . . . Holy . . . Holy . . . Holy is the Lord of Hosts. Holy is the God of the angels."

Never had Isaiah seen beauty such as he saw in heaven; nothing on earth could compare. Now God was showing Isaiah a greater throne, a greater glory, a greater power; God was telling Isaiah that His glory was much greater than that of any earthly king. God was giving the young courtier a new vision. Isaiah needed to look at the future of God's people through God's eyes, not through his own discouraged eyes, nor through the eyes of Uzziah.

High in heaven, God sat on His throne. His robe and train flowed from His shoulders down to earth, down to the Temple, down into the holy of holies. Never had Isaiah seen a royal train that long. It was more than fine cloth; it was the *Shekinah* glory cloud. The train from God's shoulders was the cloud that extended from heaven to earth, all the way down to the mercy seat that covered the Ark of the Covenant. The Shekinah glory cloud was the presence of God Himself in the Temple, a cloud of glory by day and a pillar of fire by night. The experience was too much for Isaiah. He began to shake all over with fear, his mind panicked, and his mouth dried.

Isaiah put his hands to his face and began to cry. "My lips are too unclean for God; I live among a people that are too unclean to be God's people. I know I'm unclean because I've seen the King of Heaven. I have seen the God of the angels."

Isaiah had boasted to his family of Judah's greatness when he attended King Uzziah's throne room. Now he could no longer boast of an earthly king's greatness, nor was he proud of his identification with Uzziah's accomplishments. He had been broken with a vision of God's glory and his own sinfulness.

An angel flew to the brazen altar at the entrance to the Temple. This was the altar where lambs were killed and blood was sacrificed for sins. The death of a lamb became a substitute for punishment of the sinner. The blood became the basis of cleansing. The angel took a burning coal off the altar with the long-handled tongs used in sacrifice and then flew from the altar to Isaiah, bringing the red glowing ember with him. The angel touched Isaiah's mouth with the hot coal, saying, "This coal has touched your mouth; your sin is forgiven."

Isaiah surrendered to God. He felt ashamed, he felt broken, but, more importantly, he felt clean. Then the Lord spoke from His throne: "Whom shall I send, and who will go for us?"

Isaiah knew God was speaking to him, and it was not an idle question. The question God asked was simple, direct and demanding: "Will you go for Me; will you serve Me?"

"Here am I," Isaiah answered without hesitation. "Send me."

God told Isaiah that he would be sent as a spokesman—God's mouthpiece—to the people of God. "Go tell my people that they will hear this message, but not understand it. Tell them they shall see My work but not understand it." God was telling Isaiah that he would speak for Him, but no one would listen. God was telling Isaiah that he would fail because the people would reject him, that the nation was prosperous but spiritually bankrupt. God was going to use a foreign nation to punish them. God further explained to Isaiah, "They will reject your message of coming punishment. They are blind to see it and deaf to hear it. Their heart is too hard to receive it."

God's people believed they were above punishment. They believed the Temple made them invincible. They believed the covenant automatically protected them from danger. They believed the God of Israel would fight for them. They felt untouchable, not realizing they were only outwardly obeying rituals, but inwardly had rejected God. They worshiped Baal, and behind closed doors broke the commandments of God. Their sin blinded their eyes to the true meaning of the law. Their iniquity prohibited them from understanding the true meaning of the Scriptures.

Isaiah understood his impossible task, but he had one question for God: "How long shall I speak?" Was it futile to continue in his ministry when the people rejected him? Isaiah wanted to know if the people would eventually listen to him. Should he quit speaking to the people when they rejected his message?

"Keep speaking," God told him. "Don't stop giving the message of punishment until the land is punished . . . until the enemy drives the people from their houses . . . until the land is entirely desolate."

"But Lord," Isaiah pleaded for understanding, "if You drive Your people out, what about Your promises that Israel shall dwell in the land?"

God then gave to Isaiah a message of hope for the distant future. He told him that Israel would return to the Promised Land. God's message to Israel through Isaiah was, "I will judge My people, but they shall return from the four corners of the earth to dwell in the land of promise in the future kingdom of David."

AFTER THE ENCOUNTER

Isaiah's encounter with God was the beginning of his prophetic ministry. He went on to preach that the Assyrians were going to be used by God to judge Israel (see Isa. 1—35) and that Babylon would be used by God to judge Judah (see 40–66). God used Isaiah to help King Hezekiah pray for God's protection when Assyria, under Sennacherib, attacked Jerusalem. Isaiah predicted that Babylon would capture God's people almost 100 years before it happened. Isaiah is called the Prince of Prophets because his writing represented the most beautifully penned messages in the Old Testament.

What We Can Learn from Isaiah's Encounter with God

1. *God can encounter us when our dreams collapse.* Isaiah put his dreams in a successful king and a glorious kingdom. He wrongly thought spiritual prosperity was identified with financial prosperity. When Isaiah's dreams collapsed, God had a task for him to do. God showed Isaiah that He was going to give Israel a much greater kingdom than what the prophet had envisioned.

   Often our dreams are involved in self-interest— things we want to do, things we want to become and things we want to control. However, when our dreams collapse, where can we turn? When we come to the end of ourselves, that is when we can encounter God. Therefore, when your dreams collapse, go to the house of God where you can encounter the Lord. See Him high and lifted up in His church. Listen for His voice and what He would have you do. When your day seems darkest because your dreams are farthest away, it could be the beginning of the brightest moment of your life. God may be right around the corner.

WHERE THERE IS NO VISION, THE PEOPLE PERISH.

PROVERBS 29:18, *KJV*

2. *We are never so important that we can break God's rules in serving Him.* Uzziah was a great king who accomplished much, but he felt he was more important than his office. His problem was that he thought he was more important than the rules by which he served God. God punished him with leprosy and removed him from the office. Although he was buried with the kings in the tombs of Jerusalem, he lost his days of influence because of his sin.

I KEEP MY BODY IN SUBMISSION, SO THAT WHEN I PREACH CHRIST TO OTHERS, I DON'T BECOME A CASTAWAY.

I CORINTHIANS 9:27, AUTHOR'S PARAPHRASE

3. *When we have an inflated opinion of our self-importance, God breaks us in an encounter to prepare us for service.* Isaiah was a successful courtier in the kingdom of Uzziah when God encountered him to show him his sin. As God had to break the pride of Isaiah, in contrast God had to encourage Jeremiah and Gideon because they had weak self-worth. In God's encounter, He meets us where we are, deals with us according to our needs and lifts us to where we can serve Him.

EVEN SO YOU ALSO OUTWARDLY APPEAR RIGHTEOUS TO MEN, BUT INSIDE YOU ARE FULL OF HYPOCRISY AND LAWLESSNESS.

MATTHEW 23:28

4. *When we are cleansed of sin, we are equipped for service.* Isaiah was a servant of the human king, but he was not qualified to be a servant of the divine King. God had to cleanse him first by dealing with his sin. Then Isaiah was qualified to serve the Lord.

HE WHO COVERS HIS SINS WILL NOT PROSPER, BUT WHO-
EVER CONFESSES AND FORSAKES THEM WILL HAVE MERCY.
PROVERBS 28:13

5. *The Church is the Body of Christ, and God encounters us where His presence is manifested in His sanctuary.* Isaiah was in the Temple when he saw God, high and lifted up. Whereas God can reveal Himself to His servants at any place, such as the Isle of Patmos, under an oak tree, on top of Sinai or on a hill in Judea, God has set apart certain places where He usually reveals Himself: His Tabernacle/Temple in the Old Testament and His church in the New Testament. While some people attend church but miss God, it is probably because they have looked for Him wrongly, or their eyes were blinded. However, the church is still the best place to find God when we search for Him properly—when we search for Him with our whole heart.

MY SOUL HAS A DEEP DESIRE TO BE IN THE COURTS
OF THE LORD'S HOUSE, BECAUSE I MEET GOD
IN THE SANCTUARY.
PSALM 84:2, AUTHOR'S PARAPHRASE

6. *We must faithfully carry out our task, whether or not we are successful.* God told Isaiah that he would fail, that the people would not understand his message and would not respond. But fear of failure did not deter Isaiah from his task. His faithfulness did not depend on the effectiveness of his ministry but upon his vision of God.

SHALL THE CLAY POT SAY TO THE POTTER,
WHY ARE YOU MAKING ME LIKE THIS?
ISAIAH 45:9, AUTHOR'S PARAPHRASE

Take-Aways

- I can get a fresh dream of ministry by encountering God.
- When I encounter God I understand that I must serve Him on His terms.
- I understand my sinfulness by encountering God.
- When I encounter God, I am cleansed of sin and equipped for service.
- I can encounter God where His presence is most often manifested—in His sanctuary.
- I must carry out the task God assigns me when I encounter Him.

NOSE-TO-THE-GROUND HUMILITY*

ADRIAN ROGERS

PASTOR, BELLEVUE BAPTIST CHURCH

MEMPHIS, TENNESSEE

I am not sure exactly how the "germ-thought" that God might want me to preach got into my heart. But I found it there. "Lord, do You really want me to preach?" I would ask Him. As a high-school football player, I was not afraid of much that moved on the gridiron, but the thought of being a public speaker was disturbing. More candidly, it scared me to death.

Yet, this little seed of a thought would not go away. For weeks I would pray like this: "Lord, I think You want me to preach." Then for days I would pray, "Lord, if You don't want me to preach, You had better let me know." Finally it was, "Lord, You are calling me, and I know it."

I made a public commitment, and it was settled. From that point on I did not look back. I was thrilled—and still am—that God would call me to serve Him. My high-school sweetheart, who is now my wife, was also thrilled. In her heart, she sensed God calling her into His full-time service as well.

As a would-be preacher, I knew I needed God's might and power in my life. I also knew I was totally inadequate. I had not heard much about the power of God available to the Christian, but I knew I needed something.

Our home was near the field where we practiced football. I went alone to that field one night to seek the Lord. It was a beautiful South Florida summer night. I walked and prayed, "Lord Jesus, I want You to use me." Then, wanting to humble myself before Him, I stretched out prostrate, face down on the grass and said, "Lord Jesus, I am Yours. Please use me." That still did not seem low enough. So I made a hole in the dirt and placed my nose into it. "Lord Jesus, I am as low as I know how to get. Please use me."

Something happened in my life that night. I didn't have ecstasies or a vision of any kind, but there was a transformation. At that time, I knew very little theology. God graciously released His power into my young heart and life. There was a great joy present and a desire to share Christ with everyone.

Shortly after that time, I entered college and was asked to serve as pastor of a small country church. I was 19 years of age and utterly untrained. I am sure my preaching was greatly lacking in form and content, but God graciously and visibly worked.

I was often surprised at His power. There were commitments for repentance and tears of joy from the start in that little congregation. People were brought to Christ in unusual numbers for such a small church and town. There was no mistaking the mighty hand of God.

* Elmer Towns, *Understanding the Deeper Life* (Old Tappan, NJ: Revell, 1988), pp. 227, 228.

CHAPTER 7

JEREMIAH:
WEEPING FOR GOD

ENCOUNTER: TO BE BUILT UP FOR A CALL TO SERVICE
PLACE: IN HIS HOMETOWN,
THREE MILES NORTHWEST OF JERUSALEM
SCRIPTURE: JEREMIAH 1

The high priest adjusted his scepter, wanting his headgear to be at the right angle. Hilkiah was wearing the high priestly clothes—all of the official wear—to impress the young king. He was only one among many standing in line for an audience with the new king. Hilkiah thought as he stood in line, *This eight-year-old king's advisors are all evil and will make the king as evil as his father.* He prayed that his scheme to bring revival to Israel would work.

"Next," the royal page announced.

Hilkiah stepped up next to the pink marble coronation column in the great hall, the place where visitors waited for an appointment with the king. The wise high priest waited until he got the young king's eye; then Hilkiah bowed his head in reverence to the king, all the while begging God, *Lord, stop the evil counselors now.*

Before King Josiah could acknowledge Hilkiah, a friend of the king's father whispered to the young ruler, "Don't talk to the foolish priest; religious people only want more money."

"I want to hear him," Josiah answered. "What can I do for you?" the boy king asked as he held out his scepter for Hilkiah to approach the throne.

"I can help you become a better king," Hilkiah responded respectfully, grinning to gain approval. "The better you can read and write, the better you can lead your people. Israel is not the largest nation, so we cannot defend ourselves with the largest army. Israel must defend itself with wisdom and brilliant leadership. The king of God's people must be smarter than the kings of our enemies."

"Agreed," cried the young king, jumping to his feet.

Hilkiah went on to explain to Josiah that God had commanded that each king copy the Word of God and then keep his personal copy of the Scriptures at his side to guide him in making decisions and leading Israel. "You will learn as you copy. You will become skilled with the meaning of words so you can persuade other kings of your plans. You will learn to think like God." Humbly, he added, "I will be your teacher."

Hilkiah had a strategy. He was one godly man against a whole culture that had turned its back on God. There were Baal altars in the Temple; Hilkiah couldn't remove them because a former king's order had put them there. The same edict applied to the grove of trees dedicated to Baal and Ashtaroth and high places to sacrifice. When Hilkiah ordered them removed, they laughed at him. There were altars to foreign gods in the Temple that had been placed there by Solomon. When he ordered them removed—they laughed at him. Next to the Temple was a house for male prostitution. When he ordered it removed—they laughed at him. Hilkiah felt powerless as high priest, so he prayed, "God help me bring revival to our land; Israel has for-saken You, and I cannot remove sin." As he begged God for an answer, he remembered the admonition: "Train up a child in the way he should go, and when he is old he will not depart from it" (Prov. 22:6).

Hilkiah's strategy was simple. Day after day he would train young Josiah in God's way of righteousness; then, when the king grew older, he would lead the nation in revival. And so, each morning as Hilkiah read carefully from the Scriptures, Josiah sat at a writing stand, meticulously copying the Law. And the high priest prayed daily, "Lord, open his spiritual eyes. Lord, give him a desire for righteousness."

But even as Hilkiah prayed for King Josiah, he also prayed for his own young son, Jeremiah. "Lord, open his spiritual eyes. Lord, give him a desire for righteousness."

Each afternoon Hilkiah watched his son, Jeremiah, copy the same Scriptures that the young king copied in the morning. Hilkiah trained his son as carefully as he taught the king. His plan to rid Israel of sin was a double-edged sword; it involved preparing a king and preparing his son.

Josiah and Jeremiah were the same age physically, but they were entirely different in personality. Where Josiah was demand-ing and domineering, Jeremiah was soft-spoken and considerate of others. Hilkiah was concerned that his son could never be the high priest if he were not more assertive. Jeremiah was too sensi-tive, too shy, almost too withdrawn to be a leader. Hilkiah had doubts about Jeremiah joining up with Josiah to turn the nation to God.

Determined to make his son more assertive, one morning Hilkiah made Jeremiah sit in the lead desk to copy Scripture. When he returned that evening, Jeremiah had given his position to another and was sitting in the rear of the room. Hilkiah thought, *How can Jeremiah lead the nation, if he won't even lead a class of scribes?*

Hilkiah tried to give his son a vision of being high priest. Each day when the father returned home from Jerusalem, he shared the new developments in the Temple with his son. Technically, Jeremiah would be a priest in training until age 30, when he was anointed into office and dipped into the golden laver as a symbol of his cleansing. Hilkiah told Jeremiah, "When you become high priest, you will help Josiah do exploits for God." Hilkiah looked for fire in his son's eyes, but it was not there. He wanted to see a passion for leadership, for power, for office, but Jeremiah remained passive.

Hilkiah took pride in the accomplishments of young King Josiah. His strategy was working. The old high priest had trained the king to bring revival, and God was beginning to transform the nation through Josiah's leadership.

Twenty-one-year-old Jeremiah was at school practicing his letters. The room was empty, and he was more concerned with understanding the message of God's Word than with the correct letters. Then God spoke to him in an audible voice.

"Who's there?" Jeremiah responded, startled.

"I have a special call for you," God told Jeremiah. "This call is not to be a priest but to be a prophet. Before you were conceived in your mother's womb, I knew you and had a plan for you. I have ordained you to be a prophet to the nations."

Jeremiah didn't want to be a prophet because that required boldness. A prophet had to challenge people. That was not Jeremiah's way of doing things. Also, he didn't want to minister to the nations. He loved Israel. He loved the sight of Jerusalem, God's city.

There was no greater ordination than being called into service by the actual Word of God. God had chosen Jeremiah to be

His spokesperson. But Jeremiah had doubts. "I'm a child," he protested, referring to his young age by Jewish standards. "A child cannot speak; no one will listen to me."

But God doesn't sympathize with our excuses, nor does He respond to our level of response. "Do not call yourself a child," God told Jeremiah. "You will go to all the people where I send you. What I command, you will speak."

God's call to Jeremiah terrorized him. He had grown up in a protected home, the son of a powerful father, living in a community of priests. He was not trained in hard-nosed bargaining like a businessman, nor was he taught to argue like a lawyer or scribe. But God encouraged Jeremiah. "Be not afraid of their faces. I am with you to deliver you."

Then the Lord reached forth His hand and touched Jeremiah's mouth. The Lord told him, "I have put My words in your mouth with this touch."

Jeremiah read the book of Isaiah where God touched Isaiah's mouth to cleanse it. But where Isaiah had needed cleansing, Jeremiah needed strengthening. Isaiah was an arrogant young courtier who needed his selfish will broken; Jeremiah was an introverted young man who was not sure of himself. He needed God's encouragement.

"Behold," the Lord said to Jeremiah. "My words are in your mouth. My words will be a hammer that breaks the rocks in pieces. My words will be a fire that purges away sin. I have set you this day over kingdoms to pull them down and to destroy them."

But the message God would speak through Jeremiah was not just of judgment. God also had a message of hope for Jeremiah to proclaim, a commission "to build and to plant."

With the audible voice of God came a second part of the call of God. God showed young Jeremiah a vision. He saw in the sky an early spring branch from an almond tree. The new leaves were developing and the flowering buds were in bloom. Of all the trees in Israel, the almond tree was the first to bloom, appearing in late winter even before spring arrived. God asked Jeremiah, "What do you see?"

"I see an almond branch."

God told Jeremiah that the branch was a whip that He would use to punish Israel, just as a parent takes a switch to a disobedient child. Even though God's people were beginning to experience revival under King Josiah, no one knew yet that the young king would instigate a misguided battle with Egypt, where he would be killed. The next kings would all be weak, sinful, rebellious, and would lead Israel to destruction.

Then God showed Jeremiah a second vision and asked, "What do you see, Jeremiah?"

Jeremiah answered that he saw a large cooking pot boiling over, the broth in the pot spilling out from the north. Jeremiah studied the pot a long time, not understanding what it meant. Then God told him, "This pot stands for a nation, for out of the north an evil nation will pour out its wrath over Judah to punish her for her sin." Then to make sure Jeremiah understood the enormity of the problem, God explained, "I will call this nation from the north; it will enter Jerusalem and set its throne there. That nation will destroy all the cities of Judah."

AFTER THE ENCOUNTER

Jeremiah's encounter with God began his prophetic ministry. He warned the southern kingdom that Babylon would destroy them. After King Josiah, the kings of Judah put their trust in an alliance with Egypt against Assyria. Nevertheless, Jeremiah's predictions were right. It was not Egypt or Assyria that captured

God's people. King Nebuchadnezzar of Babylon defeated Assyria and quickly repelled an invasion by Egypt, allowing Babylon to become the world ruler. Nebuchadnezzar captured Jerusalem but treated Jeremiah kindly because the prophet spoke the truth about Babylon.

Jeremiah's Discoveries in Encountering God

1. *God prepares a person to deal with a spiritual crisis long before it develops.* God places kings in their office and allows them to accomplish their intended purpose. He knows those who are evil and those who are righteous long before they assume office. Since God usually deals with issues by a specific person, He prepares that person to deal with that spiritual crisis. In this chapter, two young men are being prepared to intervene against evil. Josiah was the son of an evil father and a more evil grandfather, but in the mercy of God, Josiah was raised up—with the influence of Hilkiah—to be a revival king. The other young man being prepared for God's purpose was Jeremiah, from the godly home of the high priest.

GOD CAN JUDGE OUR HEARTS; HE PUTS DOWN ONE
PERSON AND LIFTS UP ANOTHER.
PSALM 75:7, AUTHOR'S PARAPHRASE

2. *Some people give their greatest service to God by training a child for future service.* While the story of Hilkiah's actually training Josiah and Jeremiah is an application of

the Bible text, it is based on the influence he had through the two young men who followed his example. While some cannot do exploits for God, they can equip their children to do them.

TRAIN UP A CHILD IN THE WAY HE SHOULD GO, AND
WHEN HE IS OLD HE WILL NOT DEPART FROM IT.
PROVERBS 22:6

3. *Our personalities determine how we will respond to an encounter with God, and how we will serve Him.* Jeremiah's tenderness is seen in his self-description as a child and in his fear of public speaking. This characteristic led to his being known as "the weeping prophet" (see Jer. 9:1; 13:17). Our personalities also determine how we will minister for Christ. The tenderness of Jeremiah was used to communicate to Israel the mercy of God—He loved them even when He was punishing them. Jeremiah brought a message of judgment, but he did so with a broken heart.

THEREFORE MOST GLADLY I WILL RATHER BOAST
IN MY INFIRMITIES, THAT THE POWER OF
CHRIST MAY REST UPON ME.
2 CORINTHIANS 12:9

4. *God's calling for our ministry is greater than our choice or the choice of our parents.* Jeremiah was born in the priestly

line, but God had a greater calling for his life. God's calling is greater than our choice or our parents' choice. Our best choice is to submit to Him.

YOU SHOULD WALK WORTHY OF GOD'S CALLING.

I THESSALONIANS 2:12, AUTHOR'S PARAPHRASE

5. *Sometimes God encounters us only with His Word, not with visions or other physical phenomena.* God uses visions to call certain people to service, while a physical representation of God may appear to others. But to Jeremiah, it was the Word of the Lord. One of the key phrases in the book of Jeremiah is, "The word of the LORD came to me" (1 Jer. 2:1).

THESE WERE MORE FAIR-MINDED THAN THOSE IN THESSALONICA, IN THAT THEY RECEIVED THE WORD WITH ALL READINESS, AND SEARCHED THE SCRIPTURES DAILY TO FIND OUT WHETHER THESE THINGS WERE SO.

ACTS 17:11

6. *An encounter with God stretches us beyond our culture and background.* God directed Jeremiah away from ministering only to the Jewish people and away from Temple ministry. God wanted him to be a prophet and minister to the nations.

Susannah Wesley went to the Archbishop of Canterbury to seek ordination for her son, John Wesley. In those days, a man was ordained to the ministry of a particular church, and no churches were open when Wesley's mother sought it for him. Knowing John Wesley was interested in mission work in the land of Georgia, the Archbishop proceeded to ordain him "to the world." No one understood the providence of God in those prophetic words, for John Wesley truly went on to fulfill the words of his ordination and influence the world.

BUT YOU SHALL RECEIVE POWER WHEN THE HOLY SPIRIT HAS COME UPON YOU; AND YOU SHALL BE WITNESSES TO ME IN JERUSALEM, AND IN ALL JUDEA AND SAMARIA, AND TO THE END OF THE EARTH.

ACTS 1:8

7. *Our encounter with God can influence the destiny of nations.* Jeremiah influenced Judah, Babylon, Egypt, Moab and other surrounding nations. He had no idea how extensive his influence would be when he submitted to God's call.

GO INTO ALL THE WORLD AND PREACH THE GOSPEL TO EVERY CREATURE.

MARK 16:15

Take-Aways

- I may encounter God in my lifetime, but He planned it before I was born.
- I may do my greatest service to God through my children.

- I will encounter and serve God according to my personality.
- I realize God's choice for ministry is more important than my choice.
- I may be encountered only by God's Word and not His visual presence.
- I may be stretched beyond my culture and background by an encounter with God.
- I can influence the destiny of nations after encountering God.

A PERSISTENT VISION FOR THE WORLD*

RICHARD C. HALVERSON

FORMER CHAPLAIN, UNITED STATES SENATE, WASHINGTON, DC

I did not go deeply into sin in the grosser sense, yet from the standpoint of pride and self-determination I was certainly rebellious and insubordinate toward God, to say the least.

Six months of careless living, economic difficulty, and professional disappointment in Los Angeles helped me to see that the direction I was taking could easily lead to self-destruction. Accordingly I "dropped in" to the church nearest my residence, was readily and warmly received and soon blessed with a group of new friends whose lives were centered in the church and quite the antithesis of what I had known for many years.

Three months after I entered the Vermont Avenue Presbyterian Church, the Reverend L. David Cowie candidated for its pulpit. Listening to him two Sundays awakened in me a deep desire to possess the indefinable quality which was so obviously in him. I questioned him about this with the result that he led me to faith in Christ.

Following my conversion, there were three very definite crises which have decidedly marked my life and ministry. The first occurred five months after I received Christ as my Savior. There was no doubt of the new birth following my talk with Cowie. Within two weeks my life had unconsciously undergone a radical adjustment of which I became aware in retrospect. My motivation, affections and affinities switched 180 degrees. I was literally a new person. Very shortly the implications of faith in Christ began to grip my heart and the conviction crystallized and deepened that God had a very definite plan for my life. Though I was not willing to admit it even to myself, I felt this involved the mission field, evangelism, or the pastorate.

Awareness that God had a plan for my life became increasingly urgent upon me. The second crisis came at a Mount Hermon conference near San Jose. My burden and bewilderment increased steadily during the first three days of the conference until finally I requested my pastor's permission to return home. The wise preacher consented on the provision that I would try just one more day at the conference. To this I agreed and was inwardly preparing to leave on the morrow. That evening, there were about 800 young people present I recalled, but it seemed to me that Dr. McCune spoke directly to me throughout the message. The decision seemed to involve me alone.

The issue was very clear: Christ wanted my life in full surrender. I literally broke out in a cold sweat as I realized this. At that moment surrendering to Christ seemed to mean the end of everything I'd ever dreamed of for myself. To me it meant turning my back on everything I had wanted to be and do.

I left the meeting that night in a terrible condition, having refused to yield to Christ. However I was rushed from there into a cabin prayer meeting during which time God met me in an unusual way. I surrendered to Him as completely as I knew how; and of course experienced the deepest peace and happiness I had ever known . . . when I returned to Los Angeles my church friends were aware of great changes in my life.

After I completed seminary, I was assigned to a church in Coalinga, Kansas (my first assignment). I entered into a period of disillusionment that became so acute I felt I must leave the ministry unless something happened to alter the situation. This was resolved when after two weeks of intense aloneness and spiritual wrestling accompanied by the feeling that God had put me aside for any further useful service, I finally told the Lord I was going to continue to serve Him the rest of my life whether there were any fruit or blessing in that service, and whether or not He would finally accept me in heaven. Furthermore I was willing to be "buried" for the rest of my life in Coalinga and serve in obscurity there or anywhere. This was a tremendous hurdle for me for I had become very ambitious. When this was settled, I took a completely new lease on life.

One month later I accompanied a group of our Sunday school teachers to Forest Home Bible Conference in the San Bernardino region of Southern California for a training conference. This is where the third crisis occurred. Following the evening meeting I left the group to return to my cabin. However, the way led past Miss Henrietta Mears's cabin; and here I was strangely constrained to enter and pray. As I approached the door, though the cabin was darkened, I realized some were inside praying. Not wishing to disturb them, I waited outside for perhaps 10 or 15 minutes when the absurdity of my position overtook me. It seemed logical that I should join whoever was praying inside. So I opened the door, crossed the room through the darkness to a chair I could see was empty and knelt beside it.

A long period of silence ensued and I began to feel that they were waiting for me to pray. I began to pray, others followed, and God came down into that cabin. There was no unusual ecstatic or cataclysmic experience, but God visited us in a way none of us had known before. There was weeping and laughter, much talking and planning. What is most clear from that experience is the fact that upon the hearts of us who were in that prayer meeting was laid a burden for the world and a world-wide vision that persists to this day. Through the years that vision has been fulfilled in many respects in detail as we saw it that evening; and the vision remains as fresh and vivid as ever to us.

* V. Raymond Edman, *They Found the Secret* (Grand Rapids, MI: Zondervan Publishing House, 1984), pp. 55-59.

CHAPTER 8

EZEKIEL:
SEEING VISIONS FOR GOD

ENCOUNTER: FOR A NEW CALLING
PLACE: ON A RIVERBANK IN BABYLON
SCRIPTURE: EZEKIEL 1—3

The young scribe sat at his desk stroking his black wavy beard. It was his task to make copies of important messages for the Jewish leadership. He had to copy each letter accurately. He was not yet a leader—shortly he would become a priest—yet he had no temple in which to perform his priestly functions. The young scribe lived in Babylon, almost 800 miles from Jerusalem and the Temple of God.

Young men were inducted into the priesthood at age 30. Today was Ezekiel's thirtieth birthday. This should have been the most glorious day of his life. This should have been the day when he would be taken into the Temple and anointed with blood for cleansing, then with oil as a sign of wisdom. He should have been dipped into the water of the golden laver as all other Levites are when inducted into office.

Ezekiel knew this day was the day of his birth, but he wouldn't tell anyone. How could he celebrate? He was in exile, a prisoner living among the heathen Babylonians, a captive from Jerusalem. Ezekiel was dreaming of this when his thoughts were interrupted by a messenger entering the classroom with a letter from the prophet Jeremiah.

Ezekiel's eyes glistened with anticipation. He loved to copy the letters of Jeremiah. Some of his classmates said he had even developed Jeremiah's style.

The teacher gave the letter to Ezekiel to read out loud. Ezekiel quickly surveyed the scroll, unrolling it to glance at the next panel. *No,* Ezekiel said to himself, disagreeing with what he read. His classmates saw the furrows on his brow, and they knew the letter contained bad news.

"It's impolite not to read out loud," the teacher admonished him. Ezekiel, standing beside his desk, cleared his throat and read the salutation: "To the captives carried to Babylon."

Members of the class muttered; none of them liked being held prisoner in Babylon. Heathen idols were everywhere, their food was sacrificed in heathen temples, and the dress of the Babylonians was different. Ezekiel again cleared his throat to get their attention. Then he read what Jeremiah told them to do: "Build houses, live in Babylon, plant gardens, get married, begin your families, . . ."

"No!" a stern young student's voice objected. "We will not live in this heathen land. We are to fight; we must escape!"

"Quiet!" the teacher chastised the hothead and then nodded to Ezekiel to continue.

"Seek the peace of the city where the Lord has sent you," Ezekiel read. "Pray to the Lord for His peace upon your city. Only as your captors have peace will you have peace."

Again the class erupted in protest. Again the teacher quieted them, so Ezekiel could finish reading the shocking words of

Jeremiah's letter: "You will be in Babylon for 70 years; then the Lord will visit Israel and cause His people to return to the Promised Land."

The news of 70 years in captivity stunned the class of young students. Most of them were in their 20s. They all wanted to go home as soon as possible, not wait 70 years. They would be over 90 years old—if they lived that long—before they could return to the land of their birth. Their smiles dropped; all laughter was gone. Hope is a good medicine that makes suffering easier. But now there was no hope; their dreams of going home had been snatched from them.

"Another prophet said we'd be going home soon," argued a voice from the rear of the room.

Ezekiel shook his head and lifted his hand for silence; then he read Jeremiah's warning: "Don't listen to false prophets in Babylon who predict that Israel won't be judged. There are also false prophets in Jerusalem that predict God's city will not be destroyed. False prophets in Babylon will also predict the captives will come home."

The room was silent as students glanced at one another, not daring to smile. Ezekiel continued reading. "After 70 years the Lord will visit His people to bring them back to Jerusalem."

Jeremiah's letter pointed out the rebellious heart of Israel. They were stiff-necked, lusting after idols, whoring after other religions, seeking protection from foreign nations. Then Ezekiel read the beautiful words of Jeremiah: "When God's people call upon Him, He will listen to them." For the first time since reading, Ezekiel smiled at what God said. "My people shall seek me and find me when they search for me with their whole heart."

Ezekiel was the last student to leave school that day. His tunic fluttered in the afternoon breeze as a storm brewed on the northern horizon. He had to walk about a mile to his home, where he lived on the banks of the Chebar Canal, the largest manmade canal in Babylon, stretching from the Tigris to the Euphrates River. He gloried in its engineering feat, yet was saddened that a thousand slaves a mile had lost their lives digging this canal that linked the two greatest rivers in the world.

I'm at the center of civilization, Ezekiel thought as he saw a large white sailing ship approaching on the horizon. Then he felt guilty for his enjoyment. *Jerusalem is the center of my faith . . . the city of God.*

Up ahead was his small mud-walled home. Its flat roof and small windows resembled his home back in Jerusalem. July was hot, hotter here in the desert of Babylon than living in the mountains of Jerusalem. The heat was unbearable in the summer, the late afternoons being the worst. *The storm will cool things off,* Ezekiel thought, *but it's still a long way off.*

After the evening meal, while his wife was busy cleaning up, Ezekiel went into the yard to pray. Because of the approaching storm, there were no ships in sight, and all his neighbors had gone inside to escape the sand blowing against their stalwart houses. Ezekiel was left alone to face the storm.

"A whirlwind," he mused as he saw the desert sand whip up into a funnel that sucked the hot drafts into the cool thunderclouds. The tornado danced across the desert floor, then sucked up water into a waterspout as it crossed the Chebar Canal. Then the black storm broke around Ezekiel, only there was no rain, only wind, and lightning and thunder. The clouds continued to darken.

Then Ezekiel saw it. From the center of the thick cloud appeared smoldering red fire as lightning flashed out of the clouds to the earth. In the center of the clouds Ezekiel spotted the fire, darker than amber coals, almost black. The dark clouds appeared to be smoke from the fire, only he didn't smell smoke.

Then Ezekiel saw four beings in the clouds, all looking like men, only they had wings and were flying straight at him. Ezekiel had never seen angels, but he knew immediately that the figures in the sky were angels.

Ezekiel studied everything, trying to remember what he saw in order to describe the dazzling scene that was playing out before him. The four creatures had the bodies of men and the wings of angels, yet one had the face of a lion, the next had the face of an ox, the third had the face of a man, and the last had the face of an eagle.

Next Ezekiel saw giant wheels, like chariot wheels, each taller than a tree, and each wheel was within another wheel, both turning, both rolling, both coming toward him. Then Ezekiel realized the wheels were following the four creatures with wings. Wherever the men went, the wheels followed them. When the angels turned to one side, the wheels followed them.

Next Ezekiel saw the storm cloud transform to a crystal sky. Ezekiel was no longer afraid; the experience was exhilarating. He knew God was talking to him.

Then Ezekiel heard it—a mighty roar—an approaching noise that grew louder each moment, like storm waves beating on the shore, like the stomping of angry soldiers' feet as they entered battle, like thundering horses' hooves—only louder. Ezekiel heard the beating wings of the angels against the sky as they flew overhead. Then he looked up and he saw it: the throne of God.

It was exactly as he had expected it to be, high in the sky above him, appearing to be made of a sparkling blue sapphire. What appeared to be a man sat upon the throne. A beautiful rainbow—perfect in all the seven colors of the spectrum—made the rainbow more dazzling than Ezekiel had ever seen. Like rays from the sun, it reflected the glory of God. Ezekiel fell to his face before God in response.

"Stand on your feet," the Lord said to Ezekiel. "I have a message for you."

Ezekiel slowly arose, trying to take in all that surrounded him. Then the Lord said, "I am sending you as my messenger to Israel, a rebellious nation. My Spirit will enter you and will speak through you."

Ezekiel understood that God was calling him to be a prophet, rather than a priest. The Lord told him that the people would not listen to him but that he should not be afraid of them, explaining that "at least they will know a prophet has been among them." Then God reminded Ezekiel, "My people are rebellious. You should not be rebellious."

Then Ezekiel heard a rumble, the sound of rock crushing rock, sand grating upon sand, the noise of a tremendous earthquake. The presence of God was leaving. Ezekiel heard another sound—the noise of angel wings, flapping against one another—as the angels also departed.

The Spirit then picked up Ezekiel from his house next to the Chebar Canal and took him to the village of Tel Abib, a village of Jewish captives several miles away. Ezekiel entered a house and was immediately given a room, as the occupants recognized him as the young priest intern who was training as a scribe. But now they realized that he was from God; no one questioned him.

For seven days Ezekiel sat alone in the room, in silence, in prayer and in meditation. He couldn't speak, so he didn't even try. At the end of seven days, God spoke to him, giving him a new title: "Son of Man, you are a watchman to my people Israel." God explained how the watch is responsible for the safety and protection of the people in a city. God told Ezekiel, "If you refuse to warn the people of coming judgment, I will require your blood, because they are innocent. If you warn the people but they will not listen to you, their blood will I require of them, because they are guilty. You will have done what I required of you."

God then paralyzed Ezekiel, so he couldn't go out to the people. A prophet usually went into the streets and markets to announce his message. Ezekiel was different. The elders and leaders were forced to come to him to hear God's message.

AFTER THE ENCOUNTER

After the life-changing influence of this vision, Ezekiel prophesied to the people in Babylon. He used symbols, sermons and warnings to communicate God's message to them. God used Ezekiel to remind "the whole house of Israel" of the sins that had brought them into captivity. He predicted destruction of Jerusalem and the surrounding nations that fought against God's people. He predicted national restoration of Israel to the Promised Land, and judgment upon the oppressors of God's people. He predicted the restoration of the national glory under the Davidic monarchy and the restoration of the Temple. Although Ezekiel was not able to minister in the Temple, he saw it in visions and described its future glories. His prophecies contain more about the future Temple in the coming millennium than any other prophet.

What Ezekiel's Encounter with God Teaches

1. *An encounter with God can come after our dreams fail and we don't know what to do.* The Jewish captives were exiles in a foreign land. Most of us don't understand the experiences of exiles, nor have we experienced the culture

shock of being prisoners. God's people were living in Babylon where there was no kosher food, nothing that resembled the comfortable surroundings of home. God's people yearned to go home.

Then Jeremiah's letter came telling them to settle down in Babylon, build houses and have families. He told them it would be 70 years before they could go home. Most of them would die abroad. Out of that disillusionment, Ezekiel encountered God and learned he was to be a prophet to Israel. God gave him a message of both judgment and hope, giving him a fresh dream—a dream that would launch him into a new ministry—to replace the one that had failed.

WHY ARE YOU CAST DOWN, O MY SOUL? AND WHY ARE YOU DISQUIETED WITHIN ME? HOPE IN GOD; FOR I SHALL YET PRAISE HIM, THE HELP OF MY COUNTENANCE AND MY GOD.

PSALM 43:5

2. *God can prepare us for an encounter with Him.* When Jeremiah's letter (see Jer. 29) arrived in Babylon, it produced gloom and pessimism. Many even rejected the news of his letter. However, Jeremiah warned against false prophets who predicted prosperity for Israel. God used the message from Jeremiah to prepare Ezekiel for an encounter with God.

NOW THESE ARE THE WORDS OF THE LETTER THAT JEREMIAH THE PROPHET SENT FROM JERUSALEM TO THE

REMAINDER OF THE ELDERS WHO WERE CARRIED AWAY
CAPTIVE—TO THE PRIESTS, THE PROPHETS, AND ALL
THE PEOPLE WHOM NEBUCHADNEZZAR HAD CARRIED
AWAY CAPTIVE FROM JERUSALEM TO BABYLON.

JEREMIAH 29:1

3. *God uses political and cultural conditions to prepare us for an encounter with Him.* When Nebuchadnezzar brought 10,000 Israeli captives to Babylon, he brought the cream of the crop. They were warriors, statesmen and spiritual leaders, all young and impressionable. The Babylonian leader wanted to train the young Jews in the ways of Chaldean culture, language and business. Nebuchadnezzar wanted these young Jews to administer his government among the Jews. Ezekiel was one of those captives who was brought to Babylon. In a similar move, Fidel Castro, when he took office in Cuba in 1959, sent his best young Cuban adults to Russian universities so that they could return to administer a Communist system for him.

God's larger scheme was to use Babylon to punish the Jews for their sins and rebellion against Him. One little peg in that large picture was Ezekiel. God was preparing that young Jewish man to write a book about the future millennium where Israel would be returned to the land and the Temple would be restored.

WHEN ALL THESE THINGS ARE COME UPON THEE, THE
BLESSING AND THE CURSE . . . AND THOU SHALT CALL
THEM TO MIND . . . AND SHALT RETURN UNTO THE LORD

THY GOD . . . THEN THE LORD THY GOD WILL TURN THY
CAPTIVITY, AND HAVE COMPASSION UPON THEE.
DEUTERONOMY 30:1-3, *KJV*

4. *We don't understand all we see and experience in an
   encounter with God.* Ezekiel saw many phenomena in his
   vision of God: a whirlwind, four angels, wings flapping, glowing clouds, a vast crystal atmosphere, a
   wheel within a wheel. Scholars disagree as to what
   those phenomena are and what they mean. But in his
   encounter, Ezekiel understood that he was talking
   with God; he understood what to do and what to say.

EYE HATH NOT SEEN, NOR EAR HEARD,
NEITHER HAVE ENTERED INTO THE HEART OF MAN,
THE THINGS WHICH GOD HATH PREPARED
FOR THEM THAT LOVE HIM.
I CORINTHIANS 2:9, *KJV*

5. *An encounter with God is private.* While God spoke to all
   the Jews in Babylon through a letter from Jeremiah, God
   met Ezekiel privately. There are some things in life that
   are done in public, and others that are done as a group.
   But there are certain things that are *always* experienced
   alone. Ezekiel met God individually and while alone.

WHEN YOU SAID, "SEEK MY FACE," MY HEART SAID TO YOU,
"YOUR FACE, LORD, I WILL SEEK."
PSALM 27:8

6. *When it seems as though our birth family and birthplace have predetermined our lot in life, an encounter with God can change everything.* Most born into the tribe of Levi were predetermined to serve in some capacity in the Temple. A few Levites were called to the highest office as ministering priests (see Heb. 5:4). Ezekiel met God one day and subsequently gave up his family ministry and professional preparation. Encountering God is such an awesome event that nothing in our life or vocation is the same thereafter.

HE WHO CALLS YOU IS FAITHFUL, WHO ALSO WILL DO IT.
I THESSALONIANS 5:24

7. *Just because we don't understand everything about our encounter with God doesn't mean there is no interpretation to the events.* Surely Ezekiel didn't understand everything he saw. Most Bible commentators interpret the whirlwind out of the north as the nation of Babylon sweeping down on Israel to destroy the Temple, tear down the city of Jerusalem and bring the remainder of the Jews to Babylon. The four creatures were probably angels, and their four faces may have stood for the different emphasis of each of the four Gospels: the face of the lion representing Matthew, the ox representing Mark, the man representing Luke and the eagle representing John. There are many other symbols in Ezekiel's encounter with God that challenge us to study, so we can understand God's purpose with His people.

OF THIS SALVATION THE PROPHETS HAVE INQUIRED AND
SEARCHED CAREFULLY, WHO PROPHESIED OF THE GRACE THAT
WOULD COME TO YOU, SEARCHING WHAT, OR WHAT
MANNER OF TIME, THE SPIRIT OF CHRIST WHO WAS IN
THEM WAS INDICATING WHEN HE TESTIFIED BEFORE-
HAND THE SUFFERINGS OF CHRIST AND THE GLORIES
THAT WOULD FOLLOW.
I PETER I:10,11

Take-Aways

- I can find God after my dreams have failed.
- I will be prepared for my encounter with God.
- I may understand political and cultural conditions after encountering God.
- I may not understand all my experiences when encountering God.
- I always encounter God privately.
- I can overcome the conditions of my birth by encountering God.
- I don't need to understand everything that is happening in an encounter with God.

THE SWEET TOUCH OF GOD FOR HEALING*

V. RAYMOND EDMAN

FORMER PRESIDENT, WHEATON COLLEGE

WHEATON, ILLINOIS

I began missionary service in the high Andes of Ecuador. We had been married a little over a year when I was stricken with typhus fever, and given up to die.

I knew I was dying.

How can a person know that he is dying? He has never felt that way before, nor has anyone from the point-of-no-return come back to tell of his experience. Nevertheless, I knew I was dying.

I was entirely unaware of the immediate. I did not remember that a few days before I had been in little aboriginal villages in the high Ecuadorean Andes helping the children of the Incas who were dying of some mysterious malady. I did not recall the long and painful trip on horseback down mountain trails to our home in Riobamba, nor the onset of typhus fever, nor the periods of delirium, nor my being found by a fellow American who got some Indians to carry me to the railroad, nor the all-day trip to Guayaquil in a baggage car.

I did not know that my wife had been advised to prepare for the funeral and with the help of a friend had dyed black the wedding dress she had used a year before; nor that her hosts, the Will Reeds, on advice of the physician, Dr. Parker, had purchased a coffin and arranged for a brief service at three o'clock that afternoon (since, in the tropics, burial must be made soon after death).

I did recall what my mother had told me when I was a lad. Not infrequently, when people come to die, she said, in the last few moments before they slip out into eternity they experience a complete, detailed review of their lives.

That happened to me.

With no effort on my part, nor any thought for that matter, I remembered the old homestead in Illinois and childhood playmates before school days began; Miss Grace, the first-grade teacher in McKinley School, and the other grades in succession; high school friends and scenes; soldiering days overseas.

As the flashback from memory's chamber faded I felt all alone in a vast world. If there were other human beings in that quiet little hospital room, I was not conscious of them. I was utterly alone and acutely aware that in the next instant or two I would be in eternity.

Then it was that I began to be cognizant of something strangely arresting in that place—an atmosphere, an influence, a Presence. It seemed to be on the floor but it covered the area of the room, and was slowly rising to the level of the bed. I could not turn my head to see if it was real or only imaginary; but I was sure it was now reaching me. In just another moment it began to surround me, to engulf and to cover me.

Then I knew what it was, for in those moments I experienced a sweet sense of the love of God in Christ such as I had never known before in all the years of my life. So overwhelming and stupendous was that love that the Life Beyond became ineffably beautiful and infinitely better than any possible condition in this present existence. There followed moments of such sacred, intimate fellowship with Him that it is impossible to attempt to retell it.

After the day when I waded so far out into the River of Death that I was closer to the other side than to this, there were about two weeks of which I have no recollection and can give no account. As I began to be conscious of being in the Parker Clinic, of the Ecuadorean nurses who cared for me, of my wife and the eight-week-old son who had come into our home, then it was that I was told the story behind my story.

Near Attleboro, Massachusetts, a rather small group had gathered in a Bible conference. In the course of their morning study they were interrupted by the conference director, Rev. E. Joseph Evans of Newton, Massachusetts, who told of a deepening burden of concern that had come upon him for the missionary in Ecuador, and he requested that they share the prayer burden with him. It was during those hours that, unknown to them, Mrs. Edman had dyed her wedding dress black, and Mr. Reed had bought a native coffin for me.

Since then I have met friends in New England who were present at that meeting. They have told me that if they should live to be a hundred years old they could never forget their kneeling to pray and their agony of spirit in their intercession for me. In the urgency of their petitions they forgot the lunch hour; but by the middle of the afternoon they experienced, they said, a lifting of spirit with the quiet assurance from heaven that their prayers for the desperate need 3,500 miles away had been answered.

* V. Raymond Edman, *They Found the Secret* (Grand Rapids, MI: Zondervan Publishing House), pp. 143-146.

CHAPTER 9

THE WOMAN
WITH THE ISSUE OF BLOOD

ENCOUNTER: FOR HEALING

PLACE: THE CITY OF CAPERNAUM

SCRIPTURE: MARK 5:21-43

She was pathetically emaciated, her sad eyes sunk deep in black holes; she smelled like rotten eggs. Long ago she had stopped washing her clothes because the sores on her body oozed all the time.

"Stay away!" a housewife yelled at her when she sat on a bench in front of a house. "You'll contaminate us."

The dirty woman continued her trek through the small hamlet. No one offered her water; no one offered her rest; no one cared.

"Maybe in the next village," she hoped.

Twelve years earlier the disease had suddenly struck and sores appeared. She tried everything to heal them: special powder . . . lotions . . . alcohol . . . Nothing stopped the pus. Nothing stopped the blood.

Now she was heading toward Capernaum to see Jesus. When someone had first told her that Jesus could heal her, she said He was another quack, just like the others. Over the years she had sold all her clothing to pay an Egyptian doctor to soak her in mud, then massage the impurities from her body. It didn't work. She had sold all her furniture to pay an Assyrian for a sweet-smelling lotion from India. It didn't work. Another doctor told her to roll in snow at wintertime; then she baked her skin black the next summer. She didn't get better but, rather, grew worse.

She had seen a blind man being led through her town. He kept saying, "Jesus will give me eyes . . . Jesus will make me see." Because of her previous experiences, she was skeptical; she was financially destitute and a social outcast with no friends, and she smelled bad.

"Look at me!" yelled the blind man as he came running back through her town a day later. "Behold a blind man who sees!"

Hope was planted in her heart; she began to think about going to Jesus.

Then she heard about the little boy in Nain whose body was being carried to the graveyard. She heard that Jesus had stopped the funeral to raise the boy from the dead. *Maybe Jesus really can heal me,* she thought.

She came over a mountain and saw the Sea of Galilee down in a valley. There were storm clouds rolling across the small lake, but it was dry up in the highlands where she descended toward the white houses and green trees of Capernaum where Jesus lived.

She quit trying to talk to people, just as she had given up trying to stop the blood and pus that flowed from her sores. She drank from streams. When no one was looking, she pulled a few heads of wheat from the stalks, then rubbed them together to make flour and added water to make paste. It was her only food.

She tried to stay out of public view as she entered the market of Capernaum, creeping along behind the stalls so she wouldn't be seen, all the while keeping her eyes open for a crowd of people that she assumed would surround Jesus. She spotted a blind beggar who was as wretchedly dressed as she. *I won't get close enough for him to smell me,* she thought, *and since he can't see me, maybe he'll help me find Jesus.*

Leaning against a tree out of the sun, she called across the road to the blind man, "Where can I find Jesus?"

"You're too late," he answered. "Jesus was here this morning. He preached on the seashore; thousands listened to Him. Then He got into a boat to sail to the other side. The last they saw of Him was when the storm struck. Of course, I didn't see him . . ."

Her heart sank. He had been here and could have healed her, but now He was gone. *Another failure,* she thought. She had given up praying; it hadn't done any good. She had wept and pleaded with God as she tried each new medical remedy, but nothing happened. Because nothing worked, she had given up hope. She quit trying.

Now that she had heard about Jesus, she wanted to pray again; however, she felt unable to do so. She felt dirty before God because her body was filthy. She felt like an outcast because no one would talk to her, no one would help her. Still, she felt an urge. Like a candle being lit that begins to burn faintly, she sensed a glimmer of hope. Therefore, she bowed her head as she leaned against the tree.

"Lord Almighty, I need Jesus. He can heal me. I need to be healed."

It was the first time she had asked God to heal her without lotion, without mud, without any of the other things she thought would heal her. She had always asked God to use something as a healing agent. But this time she asked God to do it just by Himself, and inside she felt an assurance that God was listening.

"They're coming back," a boy by the city dock announced as he pointed to a white sail coming toward Capernaum from the coast of the Gadarenes. Another boy yelled, "Jesus is coming back!"

"Thank you, God," the woman whispered.

A crowd began gathering at the pier long before the boat arrived. She stood with the others at the water's edge, almost smiling in anticipation.

"Phew," a little boy complained to his mother about the woman with the sores. The mother drew her tunic tightly around her waist and pulled her son to the other side of the crowd.

The boat scraped on the sandy bottom. Peter jumped out with a rope to pull the boat the rest of the way onto the beach. As Jesus stepped onto the shore, a vast crowd surrounded Him. Everyone was talking; everyone was excited; everyone was eager to be with Jesus.

The crowd pressed in upon Him. Those in the back pushed to get closer, crowding those in the front. "Stand back," shouted a Roman centurion in charge of the local garrison.

The crowd grew silent at the loud command. They recognized the Roman accent and the Roman arrogance behind the words. "Stand back," ordered the centurion. "Let the ruler of the synagogue through."

An elderly man in exquisite clothing stepped through the opening. The ruler of the synagogue had influence in the community, so Romans soldiers knew they could keep control of the people through the Jewish leaders. That's why the centurion was helping the aged Jairus—ruler of the synagogue and the wealthiest man in town—to see Jesus. But what the people saw surprised them. As the crowd moved back, Jairus ran to fall at Jesus' feet, crying, "Please come and heal my little girl!" His red eyes and trembling voice revealed his sincerity. "She's about to die."

Jairus clutched Jesus' robe as he begged; his passion quieted the crowd. He pleaded, "Her fever is so hot. If you lay your hands on her, she'll live."

Jesus didn't say what He would do, but everyone saw the concern in His eyes. He nodded His head in approval of Jairus's request. "Let's go."

Jairus led the way toward his home. The wealthy had moved to Capernaum because of its cool breezes off the Sea of Galilee and the tall eucalyptus trees that shielded the town from the burning sun. The Romans had built a wall around the city for protection, making it even more desirable for the rich, and Jairus was the wealthiest of the wealthy. Now he was leading Jesus to his beautiful house.

The woman with the sores was in the crowd following Jesus, but no one paid attention to her rags because they were looking at Jesus. No one paid attention to her odor because of the strong sea breeze. She began to lose her faith. *Jesus will heal the rich,* she thought. *But what about poor people? What about me?*

Then she remembered her prayer in the marketplace; she remembered how good it felt to smile again. And she remembered hope. She determined not to lose it.

She pushed her way through to the back of the crowd and then squeezed between people toward Jesus, getting closer all the time. When Jesus stopped, the crowd stopped. But she continued to squeeze between people until she was directly behind Him.

If I speak out, she thought, *the crowd will laugh at me.*

She was afraid to get Jesus' attention; He might shun her as everyone else had done. She knelt down to reach toward the hem of His tunic. No one saw her. She reached out with one finger, wanting barely to touch the hem, to make the slightest contact.

Then, just as she touched the edge of his clothes, the crowd surged, pushing her away. Abruptly Jesus stopped, looked at those behind Him and asked, "Who touched Me?"

The crowd was dumbfounded at the question. People were jostling Him and pressing in upon Him from every direction. Peter blurted out, "How can You ask a question like that? With all these people crowding around You, how can You ask who touched You?"

But Jesus knew the difference between the press of the crowd and a touch of faith. He knew that something—or someone—had pulled power out of Him, and He wanted to know who it was. As He stood motionless, waiting for the answer to His question, He looked from eye to eye, seeking the one who had touched Him.

From the instant she had touched Jesus, the woman with the sores knew she was healed. When Jesus looked deep into her eyes, she realized that He knew. She brushed through the people in front of her, falling at His feet, crying. "I kept telling myself I'd be healed if I could touch You," she explained. "All I wanted to do was touch Your clothes, so I'd be healed."

Jesus corrected her thinking when He told her that it was her faith that had healed her, not a touch. "Your faith has made you well," Jesus explained to her. "Go in peace; you are healed of your disease."

Even before Jesus had finished telling the woman that she was healed by her faith, a cry of anguish startled the crowd. It was Jairus. He was not yelling out of impatience, nor was he angry. A servant had come and whispered in his ear, "Your daughter just died. Don't bother Jesus any further."

"Don't be afraid," Jesus said, His words calm and soothing. "Only trust Me." Jesus and Jairus then walked together toward Jairus's home, as the subdued crowd followed behind them toward the row of wealthy houses.

When they arrived at the gate to the courtyard, Jesus wouldn't let anyone follow them into the property. After Jesus and Jairus went inside the gate to the courtyard, He motioned Peter, James and John to follow them. No one else was allowed inside.

In the courtyard Jesus met the mourners, already on the job. Because they were professional mourners, they knew that pay for a rich man's family was profitable, so they got there before the father could return home. When they saw Jairus, they cried all the louder.

"Why are you weeping and making this commotion?" Jesus asked. "The daughter is only asleep."

The mourners laughed at Jesus, but He demanded they leave the premises. Then He motioned to the father and mother to show Him where the little girl was located. They led Jesus into an inner bedroom where the three disciples followed Him into the darkened room.

Jesus walked to the lifeless body and took her by the hand. Then He spoke. "I say to you, get up."

She lifted her hands to her eyes as a little girl waking up in the morning and then sat up in bed. Jesus took her by the hand and she walked around the room. The parents were astonished, speechless. They hugged their little daughter.

"Don't tell anyone what happened here," Jesus instructed those in the room. The parents and disciples nodded their heads in approval. Then Jesus instructed them, "Give her something to eat." He smiled. "Little girls like to eat."

AFTER THE ENCOUNTER

This miracle took place on what is called "The Long Day," a busy day in the life of Jesus. The day began in Capernaum where Jesus talked to family members and then preached the well-known sermon by the sea that included the parable of the sower, among others. Jesus left Capernaum to cross the Sea of Galilee where He stilled a storm. On the other side, Jesus cast the devils out of the man from Gadara; in response, the residents drove Jesus from the area. When Jesus returned, He healed the woman with the issue of blood and raised Jairus's daughter from the dead. This day in the life of Jesus is included to reveal the different types of miracles done by the Savior in one long day of ministry.

Lessons to be Learned from a Healed Woman

1. *Because God can do anything, He can heal anyone, at any time, at any place.* In one sense we will all die. The Scriptures tell us, "It is appointed for men to die once" (Heb. 9:27). All people will die. But many put God in a box, suggesting He can't heal because aging, as well as the progress of certain diseases, is inevitable. But Jesus, who raised the dead, cleansed lepers and gave sight to the blind, can still do miracles today. Certainly there are limitations to medicine, and there are restraints in our frail human bodies; but let's make sure the limitations are not put on God. God can do anything; remember what He told 99-year-old Abraham and 89-year-old Sarah about giving birth to a child: "Is anything too hard for the LORD?" (Gen. 18:14).

BEHOLD, GOD *IS* MIGHTY, BUT DESPISES NO ONE; HE IS
MIGHTY IN STRENGTH OF UNDERSTANDING.
JOB 36:5, AUTHOR'S EMPHASIS

2. *To be healed, some people will try anything except God.* The woman in the story had been sick for 12 years. The physician Luke was kind in describing her as one "who had spent all her livelihood on physicians and could not be healed by any" (Luke 8:43). But Mark goes a step farther, pointing out that physicians, rather than helping her, had left her in a worse condition: "[She] had suffered many things from many physicians. She had spent all that she had and was no better, but rather grew worse" (Mark 5:26). There are different ways that God heals today. Sometimes God heals by physicians through medicines. Other times, God heals by faith in response to prayer. At still other times, healing comes through faith and prayer, plus the use of physicians and medicines. But in this story, the fact that Jesus told her, "Your faith has made you well" (v. 34) shows us that when she was finally healed, it was by faith alone, not by medicine or by physicians. In addition, the faith that heals one person can encourage and inspire faith in others.

THEN JESUS SAID TO HIM,
"GO YOUR WAY; YOUR FAITH HAS MADE YOU WELL."
MARK 10:52

3. *We can be healed by an encounter with Christ.* There are many stories in the life of Jesus where He encounters sick people to heal them of their infirmities. Whether they suffered from palsy, blindness, leprosy or other diseases, they were healed when they met Jesus.

However, Jesus heals in more than just a physical way. The woman who came to Jesus to be healed of her flow of blood also received a new purpose in life when Jesus commanded her, "Go in peace" (5:34).

A CERTAIN BLIND MAN SAT BY THE ROAD BEGGING. . . .
AND HE CRIED OUT, SAYING, "JESUS, SON OF DAVID,
HAVE MERCY ON ME!" . . . JESUS STOOD STILL AND . . .
ASKED HIM, . . . "WHAT DO YOU WANT ME TO DO FOR
YOU?" HE SAID, "LORD, THAT I MAY RECEIVE MY SIGHT."
THEN JESUS SAID TO HIM, "RECEIVE YOUR SIGHT;
YOUR FAITH HAS MADE YOU WELL."
LUKE 18:35,38,40-42

4. *Some people are not healed when they want it.* Obviously, God has a greater plan than healing for every person. Sometimes God is glorified in the death of His saints. In the story, the little girl was allowed to die before Jesus did anything. There will be other times when good people die, and we don't understand why they weren't healed. But in God's perfect plan, not everyone is healed.

PRECIOUS IN THE SIGHT OF THE LORD IS
THE DEATH OF HIS SAINTS.
PSALM 116:15

5. *Healing comes from God, not from things.* Technically, the physician does not heal us when we are sick.

A physician removes the cause of the disease, such as germs, disease or infection. The physician may do this through surgery, antibiotics or other medications, cleansing of a wound or modification of a diet. The physician changes our circumstances, but in the final analysis, the body heals itself. However, God, who created the body, is the ultimate source of all healing.

In this chapter, the woman had placed her faith in physicians and medicines, but she had not been healed. If anything, she had been left penniless and in worse physical condition than when her disease began. It was only when she looked completely to God that she was finally healed.

FOR I AM THE LORD WHO HEALS YOU.
EXODUS 15:26

6. *We can initiate an encounter with God.* The woman in the story apparently surprised Jesus by touching the hem of His garment. He was not aware of her actions until "immediately knowing in Himself that power had gone out of Him, [He] turned around in the crowd and said, 'Who touched My clothes?'" (Mark 5:30).

On some occasions God has initiated an encounter, as He did with Abraham, Gideon, Isaiah, Jeremiah, Ezekiel and Paul. However, there are other occasions where people initiate the encounter. Such was the faith persistence of Abraham and Moses. This woman also displayed such faith persistence, as evidenced in Jesus' words: "Daughter, your faith has made you well. Go in peace, and be healed of your affliction" (v. 34).

YOU WILL SEEK ME AND FIND ME,
WHEN YOU SEARCH FOR ME WITH ALL YOUR HEART.
JEREMIAH 29:13

7. *A public confession of healing is sometimes necessary.* In this story the woman apparently tried to remain anonymous by touching only the hem of His garment. But Jesus didn't allow her to remain unknown. "He looked around to see her who had done this thing" (Mark 5:32). Some churches practice the altar call, asking people to come to the front to receive Christ, or they are invited to an altar for prayer; a few churches invite people to come to the altar to pray for healing. While this practice is probably more widespread than some think, some people criticize the experience, saying it focuses undue attention on reluctant or fearful people. However, Jesus focused attention on a reluctant woman, knowing she needed His pronouncement for three reasons. First, the legalistic Jewish society that had ostracized her because of her disease needed to give her full acceptance back among the people; Jesus did that by telling them she was healed. Second, He needed to correct any false thinking in her mind. She thought she was healed because of her touch, when actually it was her faith that healed her. Third, she needed an improved self-image and self-acceptance. He did this when He told her to go in peace.

DAUGHTER, YOUR FAITH HAS MADE YOU WELL.
GO IN PEACE, AND BE HEALED OF YOUR AFFLICTION.

MARK 5:34

Take-Aways

- I can be healed by God, anytime, anyplace.
- I need faith to be healed by God.
- I can seek an encounter with Christ for healing.
- I may not always be healed.
- I recognize that when healing comes, it is always from God.
- I can be the one to initiate an encounter with God.
- I understand that after a healing encounter with God, a public confession of healing is sometimes necessary.

SEEING CHRIST AMONG THE CHILDREN*

AMY CARMICHAEL

FIFTY-FIVE YEARS A MISSIONARY IN INDIA;

CONSIDERED THE MOTHER TERESA OF THE 1800S

BECAUSE OF HER VAST WORK WITH CHILDREN IN INDIA

It was a dull Sunday morning in Belfast. My brothers and sisters
and I were returning with our mother from church when we met

a poor pathetic old woman who was carrying a heavy bundle. We had never seen such a thing in Presbyterian Belfast on Sunday, and, moved by sudden pity, my brothers and I turned with her, relieved her of the bundle, took her by her arms as though they had been handles, and helped her along. This meant facing all the respectable people who were, like ourselves, on their way home. It was a horrid moment. We were only two boys and a girl, and not at all exalted Christians. We hated doing it. Crimson all over, we plodded on, a wet wind blowing us about, and blowing, too, the rags of that poor old woman, till she seemed like a bundle of feathers and we unhappily mixed up with them. But just as we passed a fountain, recently built near the kerbstone, this mighty phrase was suddenly flashed as it were through the grey drizzle:

"Gold, silver, precious stones, wood, hay, stubble; every man's work shall be made manifest; for the day shall declare it, because it shall be revealed by fire; and the fire shall try every man's work of what sort it is. If any man's work abide . . ."

I turned to see the voice that spoke with me. The fountain, the muddy street, the people with their politely surprised faces, all this I saw, but nothing else. The blinding flash had come and gone, the ordinary was all about us. We went on. I said nothing to anyone, but I knew that something had happened that had changed my life's values. Nothing could ever matter again but the things that were eternal. That afternoon I shut myself in my room, talked to God, and settled once and for all the pattern of my future life.

She was called by the Lover of little children to the rescuing of girls from the temple, and later of boys in danger. Few missionaries or Indian Christians were in sympathy with her. Of this she wrote: "Sometimes it was as if I saw the Lord Jesus Christ kneeling alone, as He knelt long ago under the olive trees. The trees were tamarind now, the tamarinds that I see as I look up from this writing. And the only thing that one who cared could do, was to go softly and kneel down beside Him, so that He would not be alone in His sorrow over the little children."

*   V. Raymond Edman, *They Found the Secret* (Grand Rapids, MI: Zondervan Publishing House, 1984), pp. 33, 34.

CHAPTER 10

MARY MAGDALENE:
TAUGHT BY CHRIST

ENCOUNTER: TO LEARN SPIRITUAL RELATIONSHIP
PLACE: IN THE GARDEN EARLY EASTER MORNING
SCRIPTURE: JOHN 20:11-18

The dew had dampened the leaves in the garden, making it difficult to walk between the bushes without getting wet. The shadows were still black, and the eastern sky was just beginning to lighten the coming daybreak.

"Don't drop the vessel with the oil," one of the women whispered, afraid of being overheard but also afraid of spilling the sweet-smelling mixture of herbs and spices.

"The oil is expensive," the other added. "Nothing but the best for the Master."

Four women were creeping through the dark shadows of the garden toward the tomb where Jesus had been buried. They knew they were in the right garden because they had watched them take Jesus' body down from the Cross. They followed

Joseph of Arimathaea and Nicodemus as they carried the corpse into the garden, where they laid His body in a new tomb.

From a nearby hill, they kept watch until the Roman soldiers arrived. When the soldiers sealed the tomb, the women couldn't get in to anoint the Master's body with oil and spices. As the sun fell behind the horizon, the women rushed home. The Sabbath began at sundown, and they couldn't travel on the Sabbath. But now the Sabbath was over.

"Who will roll away the stone?" one of the women asked.

The first woman put her finger to her lips, shushing the others. "The soldiers will hear us," she whispered.

Three of the women shook with fear. They knew there were Roman soldiers up ahead. All of them believed the vicious rumors about soldiers and what they did to women if they found them alone, but one of the group didn't care. She had been a woman of the streets, possessed by devils, and she had drunk deeply at the cup of iniquity. Mary Magdalene didn't care about what the soldiers might do to her because she had lived in sin. Her three friends were chaste and pure . . . and they were afraid. Knowing their fear, Mary Magdalene said to them, "I'll go by myself. You three stay back in case there is danger. I will ask the soldiers if we can go into the tomb to anoint Jesus' body."

Mary Magdalene left the three women hiding behind a large rock, near the path into Jerusalem. If trouble erupted, they could run for help. Mary crept silently to the edge of the camp of the Roman soldiers, listening for human voices.

Nothing!

A bird chirped, welcoming the early Sunday morning, but no human sounds—no scraping of breakfast pots, no fires crackling, no men snoring, just silence.

Mary separated two branches to observe their camp. Nothing was there: no weapons, no clothing, no soldiers. She stepped into the clearing and then checked her bearings to make sure this was the correct garden. It was. She thought about the gigantic stone at the mouth of the tomb. She looked toward the stone to see how much it actually weighed. She couldn't believe her eyes! The tomb was open, and the stone was rolled away.

She ran to the tomb to search for the body. Although it was still dark, she could see enough to know that the body of her Lord was not there. "It's gone," she spoke out loud to no one. "They've taken His body."

Mary began a wild dash to the city, forgetting about her three friends hiding behind the big rock, thinking only that she must tell Peter and John. Surely they would find Jesus' body.

Within a few minutes, Mary had awakened Peter and John and told them that someone had taken the body of Jesus. The two disciples raced through the early morning toward the garden. When they ran off, Mary sat down to catch her breath. Running from the tomb to John's house had winded her. She drank some water and then waited for her hands and legs to quit trembling.

What Mary Magdalene didn't know was that while she was resting and catching her breath, two incidents had occurred at the tomb. The three other women had come out of hiding and found the stone rolled away. They also saw an angel sitting on the stone. "Don't be afraid," the angel had said to the three women. "I know you are searching for Jesus. He is not here; come see the empty place where His body was laid. Go quickly to tell His disciples that He has risen from the dead."

The second event at the tomb was the arrival of Peter and John. When they got there, they didn't see the angel, nor did they see Jesus. But they did examine the shroud in which He had been buried. That's when they determined that He had risen from the dead, for no one could have left grave clothes as intact as they found them.

But Mary Magdalene didn't know anything about these events, being alone in the house with her thoughts. She had put all her trust in Jesus. She believed He was the Messiah who would drive Rome from the Holy Land. She deeply believed Jesus could rally the Jewish remnant to reestablish the greatness of David's kingdom. Then, three days ago, He had died. She had seen the mangled body on the Cross. She had seen them bury the corpse in the tomb. And her dreams had ended. Now all she could think of was that someone had stolen His body.

After she was rested, Mary walked aimlessly into the street, going nowhere in particular, and yet she found herself heading back toward the tomb. Merchants had their stalls set up, and the market was alive with shoppers. But Mary was not interested in buying anything, as she found herself inexplicably drawn back to the tomb. As Mary arrived at the garden, she stopped to listen for sounds of life. But the garden was still and empty.

Mary wept tears of desperation. They were also tears of loneliness. She loved Jesus, and she missed Him. What would she do?

Mary walked over to the tomb, even though she had looked into the open grave earlier and seen nothing. But this time she saw two men sitting inside the sepulchre, one where Jesus' head had been laid, the other where His feet had been located. The men's clothes were white.

Mary didn't realize that they were angels, for they didn't shine, they didn't fly, and they didn't have wings. She wondered if they might be soldiers, but they were not in uniform. She didn't think they could be workers because their white clothes were spotless. Could it be that these were the two men who had removed Jesus' body? She felt numb, too drained of emotion to be frightened.

"Why are you crying?" one of the angels asked.

"Because someone has taken away my Lord," she answered,

voicing her greatest concern. "And I don't know where they put Him." Then, turning around, she noticed a third person at the tomb. She wondered if he might be the gardener; if so, he would undoubtedly know where to find the body.

"Woman," said the man, pausing for a moment. When she didn't show any recognition, he continued. "Woman, why are you weeping?"

Mary's tears made it difficult for her to see. Then Jesus spoke her name: "Mary."

His voice was electrifying. The sound of her name grabbed her attention, but it was more than hearing her name—it was the voice. She knew who was speaking to her. The One calling her by name was Jesus.

"Rabboni," she said, using a term of respect and endearment, meaning a beloved master and teacher.

When Mary spoke, her speech awakened her heart—the one convinced the other—she knew it was Jesus, not a spirit, not someone who sounded like Jesus and not someone who looked like Jesus. It was Jesus.

Instinctively, Mary fell at Jesus' feet in relief. He was not dead after all; Jesus was alive! She grabbed His feet, holding on with all her might. She would not let Him go again. She would not go through another emotional battle as she had the past three days. Mary broke into fresh tears. But they were different than the tears of grief she had shed in the tomb. These were tears of joy, not sadness. Now she wept loudly, continually, profusely. Jesus understood her emotional collapse. He knew she had been concerned about His body and about losing Him.

"Don't hang on to Me," He told her. Jesus didn't want Mary's faith to be based on the physical. "I'm just here in this physical body for a few days. Then I will ascend to heaven. I will return to be with the Father."

Jesus wanted Mary to understand that they would have a new relationship in the future. She would communicate with and worship Him in the spirit, not in the flesh. From then on their relationship would be a spiritual one.

AFTER THE ENCOUNTER

In the future, Mary would relate to Jesus in a spiritual sense, rather than following Him bodily as she did before the Cross. Jesus encountered her to explain this new relationship. She then returned to tell the disciples about her encounter with the living Jesus, becoming one of the witnesses giving credibility to the resurrection (see Mark 16:9). Although Mary was not mentioned by name, she probably was one of those women praying in the Upper Room when the Holy Spirit fell on the Church at Pentecost (see Acts 1:14). The story of Mary Magdalene's clutching the feet of Jesus is probably included to remind all of us to have a spiritual relationship with Jesus.

Seven Lessons Learned from Encountering God

1. *Jesus encounters people even though they have a wrong understanding of Him.* Mary came to the tomb expecting to anoint a corpse, but instead she met a living Jesus Christ. She did not recognize Him, thinking He was the gardener. Sometimes we go to church or go about our daily duties, not expecting to encounter Jesus Christ, and then we miss Him because we don't expect Him.

THEIR EYES WERE SPIRITUALLY BLINDED AND
THEY DID NOT RECOGNIZE JESUS.
LUKE 24:16, AUTHOR'S PARAPHRASE

2. *An encounter with Jesus brings out our strongest emotional response.* When Mary finally recognized that Jesus was talking with her, she grabbed His feet in worship, probably an emotional response reflective of her previous attachment to a physical Christ.

But even though her emotions were spontaneous and sincere, Jesus corrected her by telling her to not touch Him. He wanted her to worship him in spirit and in truth (see John 4:24), which would be the relationship of all believers to Jesus during the Church age.

AS THE YOUNG DEER BEING CHASED BY
WILD DOGS PANTS AFTER A DRINK OF WATER,
SO PANTS MY SOUL FOR YOU, O GOD.
PSALM 42:1, AUTHOR'S PARAPHRASE

3. *Our love for Jesus drives us to great sacrifice and dedicated service.* Because Mary had such love for Jesus, she was willing to face danger by going to the tomb early on Sunday morning, even though Roman soldiers were present. She knew the body had to be anointed, and she was prepared to sacrifice herself in order to anoint His body.

FOR TO ME, TO LIVE IS CHRIST, AND TO DIE IS GAIN.
PHILIPPIANS 1:21

4. *Because Jesus knows us, He comes to us in our need and calls us by name.* As Mary was in the garden searching for the

corpse, Jesus called her by name, and she immediately recognized Him and then fell at His feet and worshiped Him. When Jesus encounters us, He knows our emotional nature, as well as what we are thinking. He also knows us by name, and will come and minister to us in our need.

HE CALLS HIS OWN SHEEP BY NAME.

JOHN 10:3

5. *Today Jesus wants us to encounter Him spiritually, not physically.* Perhaps God is using the encounter between Mary and Jesus to teach all Christians the proper response to Jesus Christ. Many are like Thomas, who will not believe unless they can place their finger into the wounds in His hands and place their hands into His side. That is not the basis for our relationship to Jesus Christ today. He sits at the right hand of the Father (see Heb. 10:12), and we relate to Him because He is in our hearts, because He is in the Church, because He is in the world; we relate to Him spiritually. While we would like to grab His feet in worship and adoration, we can do that only spiritually, in prayer and worship of Him. He wants us to worship Him with all our hearts, just as Mary did.

EYE HAS NOT SEEN, NOR EAR HEARD, NOR HAVE ENTERED INTO THE HEART OF MAN THE THINGS WHICH GOD HAS PREPARED FOR THOSE WHO LOVE HIM.

I CORINTHIANS 2:9

6. *An encounter with Jesus produces a responsibility to go and tell others.* After Mary met Jesus Christ and was corrected concerning her response to Him, He told her to go and tell others what she had experienced. Later, in Mark 16:9, Mary's encounter with Jesus became one of the proofs of credibility of the resurrection of Jesus Christ from the dead. Because Mary was faithful in carrying out the task Jesus gave her after the encounter, we have another demonstration of proof that Jesus, in fact, did rise from the dead.

THE ANGEL ANSWERED AND . . . SAID, COME, SEE. . . .
GO QUICKLY, AND TELL . . .
MATTHEW 28:5-7, *KJV*

7. *Jesus comes to us in our hour of need and encounters us personally.* Mary was willing to do anything and to go anywhere to serve Jesus Christ. The Lord knew that, and when she returned to the garden, Jesus encountered her. At her moment of deepest need, the Lord came to give her a reason for living and serving. In the same way, God knows our deepest needs and comes to us and helps us through our problems.

HE WHO HAS MY COMMANDMENTS AND KEEPS THEM,
IT IS HE WHO LOVES ME. AND HE WHO LOVES ME WILL
BE LOVED BY MY FATHER, AND I WILL LOVE HIM AND
MANIFEST MYSELF TO HIM.
JOHN 14:21

Take-Aways

- I can encounter Christ even though I don't know everything about Him.
- I have the strongest emotional response when encountering Christ.
- I make my greatest sacrifices to Christ because of my love for Him.
- I am known personally by Christ.
- I will encounter Christ spiritually, not physically.
- I will want to tell others because I have encountered Christ.
- I can have my needs met by encountering Him personally.

THE POWER
TO PREACH*

DWIGHT LYMAN MOODY

EVANGELIST

I can myself go back almost twelve years and remember two holy women who used to come to my meetings. It was delightful to see them there, for when I began to preach, I could tell by the expression of their faces they were praying for me. At the close of the Sabbath evening services they would say to me, "We have been praying for you." I said, "Why don't you pray for the people?"

They answered, "You need power."

I need power, I said to myself. *Why I thought I had power.*

I had a large Sabbath school and the largest congregation in Chicago. There were some conversions at the time, and I was in a sense satisfied. But right along these two godly women kept praying for me, and their earnest talk about "the anointing for special service" set me thinking. I asked them to come and talk with me, and we got down on our knees. They poured out their hearts, that I might receive the anointing of the Holy Ghost. And there came a great hunger into my soul. I knew not what it was. I began to cry as I never did before. The hunger increased. I really felt that I did not want to live any longer if I could not have this power for service. I kept on crying all the time that God would fill me with His Spirit. Well, one day, in the city of New York—O, what a day! I cannot describe it; I seldom refer to it; it is almost too sacred an experience to me. Paul had an experience of which he never spoke for fourteen years. I can only say, God revealed Himself to me, and I had such an experience of His love that I had to ask Him to stay His hand.

I went to preaching again. The sermons were not different; I did not present any new truths, and yet hundreds were converted. I would not be placed back where I was before that blessed experience if you would give me all Glasgow.

---

* Elmer Towns, *Understanding the Deeper Life* (Old Tappan, MI: Zondervan Publishing House, 1984), pp. 224, 225.

CHAPTER 11

PETER:
A BACKSLIDER RESTORED TO SERVICE

ENCOUNTER: TO BE RESTORED TO SERVICE

PLACE: ON A BEACH ALONG THE SEA OF GALILEE

SCRIPTURE: JOHN 21:1-17

His red beard fluttered in the breeze coming off the lake. The heavy clouds over the Sea of Galilee blocked any afternoon sun. The gray day reflected Peter's attitude, as he had not had many sunny days since Jesus arose from the dead five weeks earlier.

Peter sat on the rocks to look out over the waters of Galilee. He had sat there as a boy, dreaming of the future. This favorite perch was next to the pier for the fishermen of Capernaum. As a boy from the poor village of Bethsaida, he dreamed of owning a fishing business with his family, and he did that. As a boy he dreamed of having a home in the wealthy town of Capernaum, and he did that. As a boy he dreamed of serving the Messiah who would bring His people deliverance from Rome, but he had blown that. He had followed Jesus, but when a crisis developed, Peter denied ever knowing Him.

Peter had left his fishing business with his father to follow Jesus for almost three years. He saw the miracles, heard the sermons, fellowshipped with Jesus, asked Him questions, learned from His example. He planned to be the leader of the 12 disciples who followed Jesus; he was strong, quick, and the others followed him.

Now, sitting on a rock, he thought back to that awful time when Jesus had died. *I failed,* Peter thought. *My life is a failure!*

He remembered the Last Supper with Jesus in the Upper Room; he had made a deep vow—deeper than the others—promising he'd be the last to deny Jesus or leave Him. He had even grabbed a sword and boasted to Jesus, "I will die for You. When others leave You, I'll give my life for You." And he had meant every word.

The Lord had known better. "Before the rooster crows," He had told his cocky disciple, "you'll deny Me three times."

To Peter's utter amazement, Jesus had been right. Peter had tried to follow Jesus into the courtyard for Jesus' trial, but he was intimidated by the crowd, influenced by public opinion. Sure enough, he denied Jesus three times, the last time to an obscure maid who accused him of being a follower of Jesus. As soon as he uttered his third denial, the rooster crowed and Peter remembered what Jesus had said. Then Jesus looked at Peter, and Peter was ashamed. The dejected fisherman/disciple had gone over the event in his mind a thousand times. After denying His Master, Peter had sneaked out into the dark shadows to hide, where he wept bitterly.

That was three weeks ago. Now Peter wondered, *Is my life through? Will I get another chance?* He thought about the resurrected Jesus. Peter had been one of the first to arrive at the empty tomb. But he hadn't seen Jesus, or even an angel. Jesus appeared to the disciples in the Upper Room but said nothing to Peter about the three times he had denied Him. Peter wanted to tell Jesus how sorry he was, but he didn't get the opportunity. There were too many people present. He had cried till his eyes no longer could water.

Peter was sure that God had bypassed him because of his sin, even though he knew God forgave sin. Sin was not Peter's concern; it was service. Could he ever serve the Messiah again? Peter knew he was not worthy, but he wanted to be Jesus' disciple. Peter turned in the evening dusk to see the beach where he had first met Jesus. He remembered he had been casting a net by hand into the shallow water over by the reeds when Jesus had called him. "Come after Me," was His simple invitation. "I will make you a fisher of men."

The crickets began their concert for the evening. Shadows appeared in the crevices of the rocks. Peter was not thinking of nature's beauty; he was still thinking of Jesus' words, "I will make you a fisher of men."

"That's it," Peter said out loud, though no one was there to hear him. "That's it! I'll go fishing!"

He jumped from the rocks to the path that led into Capernaum, heading straight for his house. Several of the disciples were already there. His walk reflected a new spirit as he walked briskly and with purpose. He burst into the room where everyone was finishing the evening meal. "I'm going fishing," he announced boldly. "The clouds are covering the sky, and the fish will soon come to feed at the surface." His red beard bounced with enthusiasm as he asked, "I'm going fishing. Who wants to go with me?"

Some of the disciples were also fishermen—Andrew, James and John—so they decided to go with Peter, hoping to help provide food because money was short. Also from the area, Nathaniel, Thomas and Philip decided to go with them, since they had worked on fishing boats as boys.

The lake was dark when the seven disciples pushed off from shore. The grinding of sand on the boat's bottom was therapy to Peter's frail ego. But it seemed the hand of God was against the seven fishermen. They did not catch anything. God had other things in mind besides fish that evening.

They tried all the good fishing holes, places they learned in previous years, but caught nothing, not one fish. They tried all their tricks but caught nothing, not one fish. They tried casting deep or shallow but caught nothing, not one fish.

"I don't understand it," Peter moaned to the others as the eastern sky began to lighten. "The cloud cover was perfect to catch fish, but we didn't catch one."

The sky grew lighter and a gentle mist formed over the lake, hugging the water. The breeze was gone. The Sea of Galilee was without a ripple—a glassy mirror. Then the discouraging thoughts of the seven were interrupted by a shout from the shore. Through the mist Peter could make out the outline of a man waving at them. The man shouted, "Have you caught anything?"

Fishermen are embarrassed with failure, often ignoring such a question. But for reasons unknown to the rest of them, Peter put his hands to his beard and yelled, "No. We haven't caught anything."

The man yelled back, "Cast your net on the other side of the ship. You'll catch fish on the other side."

The chords of Peter's mind remembered a similar melody three years earlier. They had fished all night but caught nothing. The Master had told them to launch out into the deep to cast their nets and then they had filled their nets when they obeyed. Peter barked orders to the others and then grabbed the nets to pull them into the boat. Almost as quickly the nets were thrown into the water on the other side. Peter obeyed the command, perfectly, instantly.

As the nets submerged into the dark water on the other side of the boat, the water churned with fish—a whole school of fish. It was as though they were fighting for an opportunity to get into the net.

"Pull!" Peter yelled as he tugged on the rope with all his weight. "Help me!" he commanded, resorting to the authoritative leadership ways of the past. All seven of the fishermen put their backs into their effort, but they couldn't get the net into the boat. The fish in the net were struggling with the men in the boat, and the fish were winning. Suddenly the youngest of the disciples let the rope go. He pulled himself up to the boat's mast to search for the man on the shore. Pointing toward Him, John announced, "It's the Lord!"

There on the shore was the Man, sitting by a small fire, no longer standing on the beach. Jesus was no longer looking for them; now they must come to Him.

"I can't wait," Peter said, reaching under a seat to get his tunic. He had been stripped to a loincloth to work with the wet nets all evening. Donning his tunic, Peter tied the sash tightly around his waist and dove into the water. With strong strokes, Peter swam swiftly to the shore. The boat, dragging the heavy net, was left behind.

Peter reached the shore and then waded through the shallow waves and ran to the fire where Jesus was waiting. The six disciples in the boat continued to row toward the shore. When they reached shallow water, Peter returned to help them, grabbing the rope attached to the net to drag it onto the beach.

"Bring some fish," Jesus told the disciples. "We'll have breakfast together."

As the sun came over the hills of Gadera, the disciples ate with their Lord. None of them had to ask who He was; they all knew it was Jesus.

Peter ate heartily, as heartily as he worked. As the meal ended, the disciples remembered the many times when Jesus had instructed them. If Jesus was going to use this situation to instruct them, Peter was ready. He found a prominent place near the Lord and then waited for a lesson or sermon. But an instructive lesson didn't come in the way of a sermon. Rather, Jesus used this occasion to penetrate Peter's heart. "Do you love Me, Peter?" Jesus asked, pointing to the catch of fish. "Do you love Me more than these?"

Peter was grieved because Jesus didn't ask anyone else that question. It seemed He was questioning Peter's love and loyalty. But why shouldn't He? Peter had, after all, denied Jesus when he said he wouldn't.

In questioning Peter, Jesus used the deepest word for love, asking if Peter loved Him as a mother loves her child, or as God loves His people. Peter felt the penetrating gaze as the Master waited for an answer. He would not brag about his love—no boasting this time. He carefully chose his answer, using the word for love that meant partnership. Peter wanted to tell the truth this time. He dropped his eyes and said, in essence, "You know I like You."

Jesus, seeing the honesty of Peter's heart, answered, "Feed My sheep."

Peter didn't know what that command meant, but he was willing to do whatever Jesus said. His heart was now yielded to the Lord. Then Jesus asked the same question again, "Do you love Me, Peter?"

Again Peter was embarrassed by the question. Jesus wanted to know if Peter loved Him enough to sacrifice all to Him. But Peter was embarrassed because he hadn't used the deepest word for love in his last response to Jesus.

Still, Peter was being honest. He knew his efforts were only superficial at best. He would not boast as he did at the Last Supper. So he responded with the same answer as before, "You know I like You."

The six disciples sat silently. Intuitively they knew they were to be quiet. They realized that Jesus was carefully leading Peter to a conclusion. He was trying to make him see something imperative. After Peter answered the Lord with the shallow word for love, all eyes instinctively switched to Jesus. They wanted to see what the Master would do now. Jesus waited patiently. Then He asked, "Do you really like Me?"

Jesus had come down to Peter's level, using the shallow word for love with His question. Peter had said he liked Jesus, so the Lord wanted to know if he really liked Him.

Peter was convicted because Jesus questioned his loyalty three times. But Peter also remembered that he had denied the Lord three times, so it was right for the Lord to ask three times. Peter's eyes lowered. He couldn't look at the other disciples, and he dared not look at the Lord. Even though Peter wanted to declare his undying love to Jesus, he knew honesty was his only option. He finally looked up to say, "Lord, You know all things because You are God. You know, because of my experience of denying You, that I can only say I like You." Then Peter smiled with confidence because he knew he spoke the truth of his heart when he said, "You know I like You."

The Lord was more pleased with the honesty of Peter's heart than with his words. Jesus had looked deeply into the soul of His disciple to see his sincerity in this encounter, and Peter had been honest . . . brutally honest. He was broken and ready for service. Jesus then renewed the commission that had originally been given to Peter: "Feed My sheep."

AFTER THE ENCOUNTER

Peter was restored to his previous place of leadership. He preached the sermon on Pentecost that became foundational to building the Church. Peter was the leader of ministry to the Jews, while Paul was leader of ministry to the Gentiles. Peter had a profitable life of ministry. Tradition says he died in Rome sometime between A.D. 64-66.

Peter's reported last words to his wife, "Remember the Lord," are certainly consistent with his message to Christians in difficult times (see 1 Pet. 2:21; 2 Pet. 3:1). When believers find themselves in the midst of difficult circumstances, taking time to consider the faithfulness of the Lord in His suffering is often enough to help them continue to faithfully endure their problems as they complete the task assigned them.

Peter's Perspective in Encountering God

1. *Good intentions are not enough to keep us faithful to Christ.* Peter told the Lord that he would never deny Him. He even boasted, "Though I should die with thee, yet will I not deny thee" (Matt. 26:35, *KJV*). Yet human strength alone was not enough, as Peter soon learned when he denied the Lord three times. Peter, of course, was sorry after he denied the Lord (see Mark 14:72). Obviously, God forgives us after we confess our sin and ask for cleansing. But that doesn't necessarily restore us to our previous place of service. Only God can perform that restoration.

THEREFORE LET HIM WHO THINKS HE STANDS
TAKE HEED LEST HE FALL.
I CORINTHIANS 10:12

2. *Some return to their old ways in backsliding.* Peter told the other disciples, "I'm going fishing" because that is one thing that he could do in his own strength. However, God sovereignly moved upon the waters so "that night they caught nothing" (John 21:3). God had a plan for Peter's restoration.

MY PEOPLE ARE BENT ON BACKSLIDING FROM ME. THOUGH THEY CALL TO THE MOST HIGH, NONE AT ALL EXALT HIM.

HOSEA 11:7

3. *Christ asks questions to get us thinking about our failure.* When Christ appeared on the shore, He asked, "Have you caught anything?" It was a question to reveal that their efforts didn't work when done apart from Him. Then, after breakfast, Christ asked Peter, "Do you love Me?" Again, it was a question that made him think about his failure. We have to think about our backslidden condition before we will do anything about it.

I AM THE VINE, YOU ARE THE BRANCHES. HE WHO ABIDES IN ME, AND I IN HIM, BEARS MUCH FRUIT; FOR WITHOUT ME YOU CAN DO NOTHING.

JOHN 15:5

4. *We do impetuous things when encountering Christ.* When Peter realized that Jesus was standing on the shore, the anxious fisherman put on his tunic, then dove into the

water to swim to shore. He probably didn't think about what he was doing; he just automatically did what seemed natural, even if it appeared illogical to others. It was an impetuous response of love and excitement.

LORD, IF IT IS YOU, COMMAND ME TO COME TO YOU
ON THE WATER. SO HE SAID, "COME." AND WHEN PETER
HAD COME DOWN OUT OF THE BOAT, HE WALKED
ON THE WATER TO GO TO JESUS.
MATTHEW 14:28,29

5. *We do extraordinary things when we are excited about Christ.* Peter swam to the shore wearing his long tunic. Then, when the boat reached shore, he ran to pull the net filled with fish to shore. This was an amazing feat, because previously seven men in the boat "were not able to draw it in because of the multitudes of fish" (John 21:6). Some say this was a miracle; others think it was simply Peter being so excited that he pulled the net to shore with a sudden burst of energy.

I CAN DO ALL THINGS THROUGH CHRIST
WHO STRENGTHENS ME.
PHILIPPIANS 4:13

6. *We must serve Christ with our talents, even though He could perform our task without us.* The Lord obviously created the

fish in the net by a miracle. There were 154 large fish, where previously there were none. When the disciples got to shore, they found a charcoal fire with fish cooking for their breakfast. Jesus told them, "Bring some of the fish which you have just caught" (John 21:10). Jesus had them add their fish to the ones already on the fire. Christ could have provided enough fish on the fire, so the disciples didn't need to add theirs. He could have waited to eat their fish without providing His own on the fire. Why fish from two sources? Perhaps the answer is in the law of the division of labor. God will do His part to assist us in serving Him, but we must properly use our talents in service.

WE THEN, AS WORKERS TOGETHER WITH HIM.
2 CORINTHIANS 6:1

7. *We can be restored to service after we honestly submit to Jesus Christ.* The Lord asked Peter, "Do you love Me?" When Peter gave the right answer, Jesus told him, "Feed My sheep." Most people believe this was Peter's restoration to his former place of leading the disciples. Because of his restoration, Peter was able to preach the powerful sermon on the day of Pentecost.

I WILL HEAL THEIR BACKSLIDING, I WILL LOVE THEM FREELY, FOR MY ANGER HAS TURNED AWAY FROM HIM.
HOSEA 14:4

Take-Aways

- I need more than good intentions to be faithful.
- I realize the pull to return to my old ways.
- I know that Christ asks me questions to get me to think about my failures.
- I may do impetuous things when encountering Christ.
- I can do extraordinary things when I am excited about Christ.
- I must fish for Christ even though He could do it without me.
- I can be restored to service by being honest before Christ.

A DYNAMIC CHANGE*

CHARLES GRANDISON FINNEY
LEADER OF THE SECOND GREAT AWAKENING
PRESIDENT, OBERLIN COLLEGE
OBERLIN, OHIO

As I turned and was about to take a seat by the fire, I received a mighty baptism of the Holy Ghost. Without any expectation of it, without ever having the thought in my mind that there was any such thing for me, without any recollection that I had ever heard the thing mentioned by any person in the world, the Holy Spirit descended upon me in a manner that seemed to go through me, body and soul. I could feel the impression, like a wave of electricity going through and through me. Indeed it seemed to come in waves and waves of liquid love; for I could not express it in any other way. It seemed like the very breath of God. I can recollect distinctly that it seemed to fan me, like immense wings.

No words can express the wonderful love that was shed abroad in my heart. I wept aloud with joy and love; and I do not know but I should say, I literally bellowed out the unutterable gushings of my heart. These waves came over me, and over me, and over me, one after the other, until I recollect I cried out, "I shall die if these waves continue to pass over me." I said, "Lord, I cannot bear any more"; yet I had no fear of death. . . .

When I awoke in the morning . . . instantly the baptism that I had received the night before returned upon me in the same manner. I arose upon my knees in bed and wept aloud with joy, and remained for some time too much overwhelmed with the baptism of the Spirit to do anything but pour out my soul to God.

---

* Elmer Towns, *Understanding the Deeper Life* (Old Tappan, NJ: Revell, 1988), p. 209.

CHAPTER 12

SAUL:
BECOMING A FOLLOWER OF CHRIST

ENCOUNTER: TO CHANGE THE MIND
PLACE: ON A ROAD NEAR DAMASCUS
SCRIPTURE: ACTS 9:1-25

The scene was chaotic. Curious spectators came running to see him die; young, zealous Levites quickly picked up rocks to join the fracas; the crowd was screaming for blood. The women were chanting, "Stone him! Stone him! Stone him!"

Stephen, a leader in the new sect known as "the way," was a follower of Jesus. Blood trickled from his mouth. His arms were raised to ward off the rocks. An open gash on the back of his head was throbbing.

The crowd was not punishing him because he was a Christian; they hated him because he had debated the teachers of the Law and won. Stephen was a Jew from outside the Holy Land, learned in Gentile logic; the Sanhedrin had not previously faced the arguments of Stephen. He interpreted the Old Testament from a Gentile point of view, so the defeated Levites beat him with their fists. As they were dragging him out of the Temple, one yelled, "Take him to the Valley of Hinnom and stone him!"

At first they were simply going to punish him, but the smell of blood in the nose of a predator spurs it to the kill. By the time they began yelling to stone him, death was the assumed conclusion in everyone's mind.

Saul, a young member of the Sanhedrin, was not at the debate; he could have answered Stephen's logic. Saul was a Jew from Tarsus in Asia, a city of liberal education and a center of the arts. Saul was brilliant in debate because he brought a fresh interpretation to the Law. Saul heard the clamor of the crowd and came running.

"Here," Saul offered to the stone throwers, "I'll hold your tunics."

Saul watched the punishing stones smashing Stephen. Some missed their mark, but no one defended the martyr, no one quieted the crowd, no one came to his rescue. The leader of the Sanhedrin arrived, and the action stopped momentarily when the elderly entourage got there. Everyone looked to the leader for permission to continue. The old Jewish leader had been hastily summoned; he was not wearing his official garments. He asked those assembled, "Has this man done something worthy of death?"

It was a question that would not be answered, at least not out loud. Saul thought, *Kill these Christians because they won't observe the Sabbath . . . because they won't bring a sacrificial lamb to the Temple . . . because they preach in the streets . . . because they do miracles by magic . . . because they claim Jesus rose from the dead.*

Saul wanted to kill this bloodied man kneeling in a rock quarry—as Jesus had been killed—but with no cross to make Stephen a hero, as had happened with Jesus.

The crowd stood, sober . . . waiting . . . ready. Then the leader of the Sanhedrin asked again, "Has this man done anything worthy of death?"

"Yes!" yelled the old members of the Sanhedrin.

"Yes!" the other members agreed.

"Yes!" shouted young Saul, glad to see a Christian die.

One stone was thrown; Stephen put up a hand to divert it. Then three or four stones were thrown at the same time; he couldn't divert them all. A rock thrown from the rear hit Stephen in the head.

Thud.

Stephen knew it was over. Already on his knees, he looked to heaven and prayed, "Lord Jesus . . . Lord, forgive their sin." Peace came over his face as he continued. "I pray for them. Save them."

The prayer convicted even the hardest stone thrower. Even those who most hated him momentarily stopped their assault to hear what he was saying. Stephen looked into the sky. He saw Jesus, though none in the crowd saw Him. Saul was interested in this man's last words before he died. A man's last words before death usually reveal what he truly believes and how he lived.

Stephen recognized Jesus, sitting at the right hand of the throne of God. Although he had not previously seen the Master with his physical eyes, he recognized Him in death because he had prayed to Him so many times. Jesus began walking toward Stephen as someone goes to meet a friend, and Stephen reached out to Jesus. Saul heard Stephen's prayer, as did everyone in the rock quarry, although no one saw Jesus but Stephen, who cried out, "Lord Jesus, receive my spirit."

Stephen died a martyr's death, but rocks did not smash the breath from his lungs; the Lord Jesus took him home.

Later that day, Saul was still at the rock quarry. He saw Christian men come with water to wash the dirt and dried blood from the corpse. They tenderly anointed it with oil and wound Stephen's body in a shroud. Saul was impressed with their boldness. He was also touched with their tenderness and love for Stephen.

A few days later Saul went to the Sanhedrin with a plan to stop the spread of Christianity. When they stoned Stephen, they had stopped the street preaching of Christians, who no longer gathered publicly for prayer. Jewish spies reported that Christians were leaving Jerusalem for other cities, such as Alexandria, Babylon and Damascus, choosing those cities because of the large Jewish populations there. Saul was furious. "Christians are going to proselytize their relatives," he announced to the Sanhedrin, speaking from the back row to the assembly of 70 men. With his fist clenched, the blood vessels on his temples popped out, and the tempo of his voice raised to a more intense pitch. "We must stop the spread of Christianity. . . ." He paused to look from face to face. They all nodded their approval, anticipating his plan.

"I'll go to Damascus," Saul suggested, "arrest the Christians, then get a letter of extradition to bring them to Jerusalem."

"You can't do that," said an old rabbi, stroking his beard. "We have no legal rights in Damascus." Several of the older members of the Sanhedrin muttered their agreement.

Another member spoke up. "We have no legal authority outside the Holy Land."

"Yes we do," Saul snapped at the old man. Saul was a student of Gamaliel, which meant he did his research well before speaking. "We have legal authority in Damascus, in Alexandria, in Babylon." Saul stopped to make his point and then continued. "We have legal authority over Jews anywhere in the Roman Empire."

Saul explained some history to the hushed assembly. He revealed how the high priest supported Julius Caesar in his battle to defeat Pompeii in Egypt in 68 B.C. In return, Caesar gave to Hyreanus II, the high priest and all succeeding high priests, spiritual authority over all Jews in the Roman Empire. Then Saul concluded, "These Christians are Jews—legal-born Jews." The group of men smiled at the brilliance of young Saul. He smiled back when he saw they were on his side. Then he said, "This is a spiritual matter of the highest urgency. It threatens the faith of Jews everywhere."

The group broke out into applause to show appreciation and agreement. But Saul didn't want their gratitude yet. He had one last thing to add. "We can't let the authorities in these other towns deal with these Christians. They won't stop them. They won't punish them as we dealt with Stephen. We must arrest the Christian leaders, bring them back to Jerusalem and let them feel the fury of the stones."

"Yes!" the Sanhedrin shouted. "Yes! Yes!"

Saul had not gone to the high priest privately with his plan for fear of rejection—rejection because he was so young. So Saul used the public platform of the Sanhedrin to intimidate the high priest. Saul wanted the Sanhedrin to pressure the high priest. Saul carried the day, the Sanhedrin agreed; now would the high priest agree? All eyes looked from Saul to the high priest.

The room sensed tension between young Saul and the old high priest. It was a generation gap between a young hothead and the older, wiser leader. The eyes of the Sanhedrin darted from Saul's face to the high priest's eyes. Would the old man approve the bold initiative? He slowly opened his lips to speak. "I will give Saul a letter of authority."

With one ingenious plan, young Saul—not yet 30 years old— became one of the leading forces in the Sanhedrin. Saul achieved authority that some members never get in a lifetime. He became the representative of the high priest and a powerful voice of the Sanhedrin.

Several weeks later a caravan of camels, donkeys and weary travelers reached the mountain of balsam trees west of the Baca Valley. They could see Damascus in the distance from the top of the hills. Looking back they could see the cedars of Lebanon across the Baca Valley, and to the south they could see Mount Hermon, the snow-covered mountain of the Holy Land.

Saul not only had a letter from the high priest to arrest and extradite Jews to Jerusalem, he had a letter of credit. Saul was riding a horse, the most luxurious of all ways to travel. He was not being bounced on the back of a donkey, nor was he being jerked about on camelback. The rich rode horses, as did army officers, so Saul used his letter of credit to secure a fine horse, one that called attention to the importance that he thought his new office demanded. His luggage was being brought by porters, again an opulent show of wealth. From time to time, Saul would ride out to high observation points to survey a battlefield like a Roman army officer. It gave him a sense of self-worth.

But all he got from his porters was the empty obedience that comes with money. They cared not that he was a Jew, even less that he was a dignitary who represented the high priest. They obeyed him for money but didn't respect him. Saul remembered the tender love that the Christian men had shown for Stephen's corpse. Saul didn't get that type of love from anyone—not the porters, not the Sanhedrin, not his fellow students at Gamaliel's school.

Saul took a white cloth to wipe the perspiration from his face and neck. Then, for a moment, he looked into the noonday sun. Its light exploded brighter than anything Saul had ever seen. He was blinded with its brilliance. But the intense light that blinded Saul was not from the sun—it was the Lord Jesus Christ Himself.

Saul's horse, sensing fear, began kicking wildly. Blinded by the searing light and losing his equilibrium, he fell to the ground. He covered his face with his hands, unable to see anything, getting sand into his eyes from his dirty hands. Saul was blind.

The luggage handlers saw the intense light. They dropped their burden to the ground and cowered in fear. They didn't know what was happening, but they knew it was supernatural. They heard a voice from heaven, but it was only noise to them; they couldn't make out the words. A voice spoke to Saul in the Hebrew language: "Saul . . . Saul, why are you persecuting Me?"

"Who are You?" Saul stammered.

"I am Jesus," the voice from heaven answered. "You think you are persecuting Christians, but you are persecuting Me."

Saul quickly processed everything in his mind. He hated Christians and was willing to kill them, just as other Jewish leaders killed Jesus. He knew Christians claimed Jesus was not dead, but was alive again. Now Jesus was talking to him. Saul heard the voice. "I am Jesus. It is hard to kick against the truth."

Saul lay groveling in the dirt, thrown by a kicking horse. Instantly, Saul knew his whole legalistic approach to God was wrong. Christians didn't just have a better system of religion, they believed in a person. They followed Christ. Saul, acknowledging for the first time the deity of Jesus Christ, answered, "Lord . . . Lord . . . what do You want me to do?"

In that statement, Saul yielded himself to the person of Jesus Christ. It would take a while to sort out his theology, and he would have to think his way through all the changes that would be required in his lifestyle. But lying there on the ground, Saul made one monumental change—he recognized who Jesus was. Though blinded, Saul had seen the light; he had seen the brilliance of Jesus Christ. In submission, Saul asked, "What do You want me to do?"

The Lord gave him instructions: "Arise. Get up and go into the city; you will be told what to do."

The horse had run away, and the luggage carriers didn't go after it because the horse was not their concern. Now working for a blinded employer, they had to get him to the city if they wanted their money. The city gate was right ahead. Taking Saul by the arm, they led him on Straight Street to the house of a Jewish man named Judah. What a spectacle. Saul did not have a triumphant entrance upon a fine white horse. Saul was being led by his luggage handlers, he had blinded eyes and dirty robes, and God had humbled him.

Saul was ugly because his eyes were ugly. Not only was he blinded, but also rubbing sand into his eyes had irritated and bloodied them. The more he tried to open them, the more intense his pain, like needles pushed into the eyeballs. Any light was unbearable. Saul squeezed them shut to keep out the light and then rubbed them until they bled. The more his eyes bled, the more Saul rubbed them, creating huge, ugly, blood-crusted scabs. Saul had been blind spiritually; now he was physically blind.

Saul, a good Pharisee, had fasted many times, demonstrating his obedience to the Law. But now fasting was different. Saul was unable to eat or drink, like someone losing his appetite when a sudden death occurs in the family. And so it was. The old Saul had died when he met Jesus. He thought, "I am crucified with Christ. When Jesus died, I died. When Jesus was buried, I was buried."

For those days Saul experienced the Cross. As a young theological student, Saul had heard Jesus say, "If any man will come after Me, deny yourself, die with Me, take up your Cross daily, follow Me." That day the old Saul died, completely.

Across town God spoke to a trusted Christian: "Ananias."

"Yes, Lord," was his answer. "What do You want me to do?"

The Lord told this humble believer to go to the house where Saul was located, lay hands on Saul and pray that he receive his sight. The Lord told Ananias that Saul had been blinded. Ananias objected. "Lord, I have heard of the many evil things Saul has done to Christians in Jerusalem. He has come to Damascus to do the same thing!"

The Lord answered Ananias's fears: "Saul is praying." Then God told him, "Saul is a chosen vessel to preach to the Gentiles. He may have persecuted the Church in the past, but he will be persecuted in the future because of his preaching."

The small room in the house was just a few steps off the street called Straight. The shutters barred any light; the door was kept closed, but light was not necessary because Saul was blind. Ugly, brownish-red scabs covered his eyes. The servant brought a basin of water to wash them, but Saul refused any help.

The darkened room had only a simple chair and table with a cup of water and some bread, but Saul refused them all. He lay prostrate on the floor, praying, sobbing and repenting. He thought he'd be blind for the rest of his life, but it wasn't his physical eyes that needed healing. It was the blind eyes of his soul that needed healing. He prayed for spiritual sight.

After three days, Ananias knocked on the door. Gaining entrance to the room, he explained to Saul, "You are my brother . . . because the Lord Jesus appeared to you."

Saul couldn't answer; he could only nod his head in agreement. Ananias continued to explain. "Jesus told me to lay hands on you and pray that you might receive your sight . . . and that you would be filled with the Holy Spirit."

Saul rose from his prostrate position on the floor to his knees. Just as he promised, Ananias placed both hands on Saul's head to pray. "Lord, heal his blindness. Fill him with the Holy Spirit. Use Saul to preach the gospel to the Gentiles."

Instantly, Saul could see. The intense stinging pain was gone. He knew something had happened because he could see in his mind, he could see in colors, he could see in motion, and he could see inside his heart. Then Saul tried to open his eyes, something he had been unable to do because of the scabs and intense pain. But now the scabs broke apart and fell to the ground, releasing their grip on Saul's eyes so he could see. What he could see in his heart, he could now see with his eyes.

Saul was saved, healed of blindness and called of God to preach, but physically he was weakened. His intense praying for three days left him in that condition. He shook with exhaustion. For the first time in three days, he took some water and a small morsel of bread. He needed strength.

Believers had gathered at the house to support Ananias and to pray for Saul. In reward for their faithfulness, they witnessed the water baptism of Saul.

AFTER THE ENCOUNTER

Saul, a Jewish member of the Sanhedrin, became Paul, the apostle to the Gentiles. Whereas prior to his conversion Saul persecuted Christians, afterward the Jews persecuted him, trying to kill him, first in Damascus and then in Jerusalem. He went everywhere planting churches, while Jews followed him to criticize, arrest, stone and attempt to assassinate him. Without a doubt, the man who encountered Christ on the road to Damascus became the most influential name in the spread of Christianity. The encounter with Christ motivated him to sacrificial service. He preached the gospel, wrote letters, trained disciples and influenced the future direction of Christianity.

What the Apostle Paul's Encounter with God Teaches Us

1. *The basis of encountering Christ is not grounded in logical explanations or empirical proofs, but rather in an experience with Jesus Christ.* Saul, who was trained in logic under Gamaliel, apparently could argue against Christianity and had rational arguments to defend his faith. However, he didn't have any defense when he met Jesus Christ. In the same manner, many atheists and skeptics who doubt the Word of God become believers when they meet Jesus. No one has to prove to them that the Bible is the Word of God, nor are they interested in arguments for the existence of God. When they encounter the Savior, they inwardly know that God exists and that His Word is true.

I HAVE BEEN CRUCIFIED WITH CHRIST; IT IS NO LONGER
I WHO LIVE, BUT CHRIST LIVES IN ME; AND THE LIFE
WHICH I NOW LIVE IN THE FLESH I LIVE BY FAITH IN THE
SON OF GOD, WHO LOVED ME AND GAVE HIMSELF FOR ME.
GALATIANS 2:20

2. *After an encounter with Jesus, our lives are pointed in different directions.* Saul was going to Damascus to arrest Christians. But after encountering Jesus Christ, he began preaching, "Christ in the synagogues, that He is the Son of God" (Acts 9:20). In Damascus, Saul did the very thing he had originally come to stop—he preached the good news of Christ.

THEN HE SAID TO THEM ALL, "IF ANYONE DESIRES TO
COME AFTER ME, LET HIM DENY HIMSELF, AND TAKE UP
HIS CROSS DAILY, AND FOLLOW ME."
LUKE 9:23

3. *People around us don't understand what is happening when
we encounter Christ.* The people with Saul did not understand what Saul heard or saw (see Acts 22:9). When we
meet Jesus Christ, we march to a different drumbeat.
Our friends who do not know Jesus do not understand
our motives or objectives. Perhaps that is why so many
encounters with God take place privately; God knows
that other people won't understand, so He often meets
His servants privately.

AND I, DANIEL, ALONE SAW THE VISION, FOR THE MEN
WHO WERE WITH ME DID NOT SEE THE VISION;
BUT A GREAT TERROR FELL UPON THEM, SO THAT THEY
FLED TO HIDE THEMSELVES.
DANIEL 10:7

4. *An encounter with God should take away our pride and humble us.* Every person wants to sit upon the throne of his
or her own life. We are all driven by selfish or egotisti-
cal goals. However, Jesus Christ wants to sit upon the
throne of our lives. The formerly arrogant Saul met
Jesus Christ and could then say for the rest of his life,
"Not I, but Christ" (Gal. 2:20, *KJV*).

BRETHREN, I DO NOT COUNT MYSELF TO HAVE
APPREHENDED; BUT ONE THING I DO, FORGETTING
THOSE THINGS WHICH ARE BEHIND AND REACHING
FORWARD TO THOSE THINGS WHICH ARE AHEAD, I PRESS
TOWARD THE GOAL FOR THE PRIZE OF THE UPWARD
CALL OF GOD IN CHRIST JESUS.
PHILIPPIANS 3:13,14

5. *In an encounter God sometimes gives us an unpleasant task.*
Before meeting Jesus Christ, Saul testified that he was
"circumcised the eighth day, of the stock of Israel, of
the tribe of Benjamin, a Hebrew of the Hebrews; concerning the law, a Pharisee" (Phil. 3:5). But in meeting
Jesus Christ, he was directed away from ministering to
the Jews to become the apostle to the Gentiles.

BUT THE LORD SAID TO HIM, "GO, FOR HE IS A CHOSEN
VESSEL OF MINE TO BEAR MY NAME BEFORE GENTILES,
KINGS, AND THE CHILDREN OF ISRAEL. FOR I WILL
SHOW HIM HOW MANY THINGS HE MUST SUFFER
FOR MY NAME'S SAKE."
ACTS 9:15,16

6. *Our friends and fellow workers may turn against us because of
our encounter with Jesus Christ.* As a spokesman for the
Jews, Saul carried a letter to Damascus for the arrest
and extradition of Christians to Jerusalem. After Saul
encountered Jesus Christ, those with whom he worked
tried to kill him, just as he had formerly tried to kill

Christians. In Damascus "the Jews plotted to kill him" (Acts 9:23). He fled to Jerusalem and there "they attempted to kill him" (v. 29). Perhaps, like Saul, many of our friends don't love us for who we are; they love us for what we can do for them and for their cause.

BELOVED, DO NOT THINK IT STRANGE CONCERNING THE FIERY TRIAL WHICH IS TO TRY YOU, AS THOUGH SOME STRANGE THING HAPPENED TO YOU; BUT REJOICE TO THE EXTENT THAT YOU PARTAKE OF CHRIST'S SUFFERINGS, THAT WHEN HIS GLORY IS REVEALED, YOU MAY ALSO BE GLAD WITH EXCEEDING JOY.

I PETER 4:12,13

7. *God has some people who will help to explain to us our encounter with Christ.* There was a believer in Damascus called Ananias who was not previously mentioned in the Scriptures, nor is he ever mentioned again. Apparently Ananias was raised up for one shining moment in life, to help Saul in his crucial encounter with Jesus Christ. Even though Ananias was initially afraid because he had heard about Saul's reputation, he obeyed God, laying hands on Saul and praying for his healing. God used Ananias to deliver a message to Saul that he was to be the apostle to the Gentiles.

SO PHILIP RAN TO HIM, AND HEARD HIM READING THE PROPHET ISAIAH, AND SAID, "DO YOU UNDERSTAND WHAT YOU ARE READING?" AND HE SAID, "HOW CAN I,

UNLESS SOMEONE GUIDES ME?" AND HE ASKED PHILIP
TO COME UP AND SIT WITH HIM.
ACTS 8:30,31

Takes-Aways

- I get proofs for my faith from Christ, not from logic or feelings.
- I will have a new direction in life after encountering Jesus.
- I can encounter Christ when people who are nearby don't know what is happening.
- I gain biblical humility by encountering Christ.
- I sometimes get an unpleasant task by encountering Christ.
- I may lose friends after encountering Christ.
- I may get help from other believers to understand an encounter with Christ.

YOUR BLUEPRINT FOR AN ENCOUNTER WITH GOD

You are on a journey called life. As you travel from day to day, you come to many forks in the road and some intersections. These are turning points that will transform your journey into a higher level of living or will point you downward. You expect some of the turning points such as marriage, the birth of a child or a new job. Some of these turning points will be unexpected, such as an accident, a divorce or the termination of a job, putting you out on the street.

You can meet God at some of the turning points. These are encounters with God that can solve a problem, point you to a new job or enrich your life by meeting God in the secret place.

Do you need an encounter with God? Suppose you say yes. Suppose you agree that you really need God. Suppose you are in a crisis and you are desperate to find God. How can you find Him? How can you recognize God at one of the turning points of your life? How can you benefit from an encounter with God?

Let's answer these questions with six handles that will help you get a better understanding about encountering God.

SIX HANDLES

You may think that only people in the past encountered God, that God met people in the Bible but He doesn't do it today. But Jesus told John on the Isle of Patmos, "I am the One who was, who is and who is to come" (Rev. 1:8). This means Jesus will live in the future, and He lives today. Christ can meet you today; that's why this book has testimonies of living people who encountered God in their lifetimes.

Encounter God Today

An encounter with God is available to all people—that means you. The young encountered God—Gideon and Jeremiah—as well as the old: Moses on Sinai and John on Patmos. Therefore, no matter your age, you can encounter God. People had an encounter with God for many purposes. Some unsaved were converted, such as Saul. Some godly people encountered Christ to worship Him. Others were encountered for a call to vocational service, for a new task, to encourage them, to break their pride or to restore them from backsliding. So no matter what problems you have in life, you can encounter God to solve your problems.

No One Is Excluded from an Encounter with God

You may doubt if the testimonies are real. Some may think these stories are made up. However, in a trial, the testimony of witnesses is introduced as fact, especially when the witnesses testify of a personal experience. Whether you agree with the content of the testimonies, the judge accepts a testimony as a fact to be compared with all other evidence presented in a trial. Sometimes testimonies are thrown out of court if there is a "collusion of witnesses" where they conspire together to tell the same story. There is no collusion of witnesses in the testimonies of this book. Those who encountered God were separated by time, geography, culture and language. They all met God, but the circumstances were different and the results were different. What is constant is their encounters with God. The testimonies in this book all witness to the same thing, which is that they experienced or encountered God. Therefore, the testimonies should be accepted as true.

An Encounter with God Can Be Real

The answer to your problems is not in an experience, nor is your focus on an encounter the important thing. It is not a "fix," nor is it a feeling. You must meet God; it is Him that you need. He has the ability to help you through your problem when you hurt or when you yearn for some glue to hold your life together. God is your answer. But almost no one recognizes his or her need of God. Yet Saint Augustine, an Early Church father, correctly analyzed the problem when he said, "Thou hast formed us for Thyself and our hearts are restless till they find rest in Thee."

Seek God

God has promised you a better life. Look in the Bible at these promises. Jesus said that we will have abundant life (see John 10:10). Paul wanted believers to be rooted and grounded in love (see Eph. 3:17). He also promised that we can be more than conquerors (see Rom. 8:37). The Bible says that God will open the windows of heaven and pour out on us more blessings than we can contain (see Mal. 3:10). Peter said we could have "joy inexpressible and full of glory" (1 Pet. 1:8).

An Encounter with God Is Good

You will find a pattern in all these encounters. Out of Elijah's deep discouragement came a new spirit of service. Out of Isaiah's broken dreams came a new purpose in life. Out of Saul's rebellion came an obedient will. Out of Ezekiel's ordinary, dull life came a new level of power. Out of John's captivity came freedom of worship. Many people in the Bible meet God, but not every meeting is an encounter that changes lives. An encounter with God in this book is defined by seven steps. Look for these seven principles or steps as you plan to meet God. The next section examines these seven principles.

Follow These Principles When You Encounter God

An encounter with God occurs when (1) He intentionally meets with you; (2) in a time of great personal need; (3) through unexpected circumstances; (4) so He can reveal something of Himself to you; (5) so you can learn something about yourself; (6) to prepare you for a specific task; (7) even though you don't fully understand all the mysterious elements of the encounter.

> *Intentional.* Some encounters are planned by God when the person least expects it. At other times, when individuals are so fervent in prayer that they won't back off, God comes to them. Jacob wrestled with God all night, refusing to release his wrestling "hold" on God. Moses would not let God send a mere angel to guide him into the Promised Land. Moses said in faith, "If Your Presence does not go with us, do not bring us up from here" (Exod. 33:15).

FOR THUS SAYS THE LORD GOD: "INDEED I MYSELF WILL
SEARCH FOR MY SHEEP AND SEEK THEM OUT."
EZEKIEL 34:11

Time of great need. Elijah met God when backslidden and
discouraged. Jeremiah, Isaiah and Ezekiel encountered
God when they saw their nation collapsing around them.
When Jacob was afraid to face a vengeful brother, he
encountered God. These problems motivated these men
to search for God. But some others were encountered by
God, even though they were in rebellion to Him. Saul
hated Christ when he met Him on the Damascus road;
Peter had denied Jesus three times. The wonderful thing
about these encounters is that when people needed God,
He came to them.

YET THERE IS ONE RAY OF HOPE: HIS COMPASSION
NEVER ENDS. IT IS ONLY THE LORD'S MERCIES
THAT HAVE KEPT US FROM COMPLETE DESTRUCTION.
GREAT IS HIS FAITHFULNESS.
LAMENTATIONS 3:21,22, *TLB.*

Surprised. Some did not expect to encounter God. Mary
came to the garden to anoint a corpse but ended up talking to a living Christ. Others, such as Ezekiel and
Jeremiah, prayed for God to bless them and were surprised by the magnitude of their encounters. Some
wanted God to do something for them, but the encounters were beyond what they expected.

THE SECRET THINGS BELONG TO THE LORD OUR GOD,
BUT THOSE THINGS WHICH ARE REVEALED BELONG TO
US AND TO OUR CHILDREN FOREVER, THAT WE MAY DO
ALL THE WORDS OF THIS LAW.
DEUTERONOMY 29:29

New message from God. When God encounters us, He has a purpose. Usually it is a particular message for us. God wanted John to write the book of Revelation. It was a simple, straightforward task: "Write the things which you have seen, and the things which are, and the things which will take place after this" (Rev. 1:19). Others needed a personal message, such as Mary Magdalene in the garden; Jesus comforted her and reaffirmed her faith.

MANY, O LORD MY GOD, ARE YOUR WONDERFUL WORKS
WHICH YOU HAVE DONE; AND YOUR THOUGHTS TOWARD
US CANNOT BE RECOUNTED TO YOU IN ORDER;
IF I WOULD DECLARE AND SPEAK OF THEM,
THEY ARE MORE THAN CAN BE NUMBERED.
PSALM 40:5

To know God intimately. God wants us to know Him intimately. He encounters us so that we will meet with Him and worship Him. "The Father seeks people to worship Him" (John 4:23, author's paraphrase). When we worship and adore God, we learn more about Him so we can better serve Him.

THUS SAYS THE LORD: "LET NOT THE WISE MAN GLORY
IN HIS WISDOM, LET NOT THE MIGHTY MAN GLORY IN
HIS MIGHT, NOR LET THE RICH MAN GLORY IN HIS
RICHES; BUT LET HIM WHO GLORIES GLORY IN THIS,
THAT HE UNDERSTANDS AND KNOWS ME, THAT I AM THE
LORD, EXERCISING LOVINGKINDNESS, JUDGMENT, AND
RIGHTEOUSNESS IN THE EARTH. FOR IN THESE
I DELIGHT," SAYS THE LORD.
JEREMIAH 9:23,24

To be changed. After we encounter God, we will be different. Meeting with God will change our lives. Jacob physically limped, an outward reminder that he saw God face-to-face and an inward reminder to walk humbly before God. Moses' face shone, Abraham received a son, Paul was called to ministry, and Peter was given a new commission for ministry.

FOR I KNOW THE THOUGHTS THAT I THINK TOWARD
YOU, SAYS THE LORD, THOUGHTS OF PEACE AND NOT OF
EVIL, TO GIVE YOU A FUTURE AND A HOPE.
JEREMIAH 29:11

Mysterious in circumstances. There are many things about our encounters with God that we will not understand. Why would God wrestle with Jacob all night before touching his thigh? How could the angels touch Isaiah's mouth with hot coals? What was the wheel within a wheel that Ezekiel saw? We do not understand everything about the infinity of God because we are finite, limited humans. There is something mysterious in the things God does. We still have a sin nature that blinds us spiritually to some of the things happening around us. Paul reminds us, "For now we see in a mirror, dimly, but then face to face. Now I know in part, but then I shall know just as I also am known" (1 Cor. 13:12). There is a mystery in every encounter with God. Perhaps God doesn't explain everything that's happening around us because He is testing our faith. He wants to know if we will trust and obey Him. He wants us to bow before Him in worship.

"FOR MY THOUGHTS ARE NOT YOUR THOUGHTS, NOR ARE YOUR WAYS MY WAYS," SAYS THE LORD. "FOR AS THE HEAVENS ARE HIGHER THAN THE EARTH, SO ARE MY WAYS HIGHER THAN YOUR WAYS, AND MY THOUGHTS THAN YOUR THOUGHTS."
ISAIAH 55:8,9

CONCLUSION

I have a pastor friend in the Episcopal church who offers an unusual invocation at the beginning of his worship services. You will appreciate this prayer as a benediction after reading this book. He greets his congregation with uplifted hands and says, "Today you can touch God . . . right here . . . right now . . . you can enter His presence and touch God."

Then my Episcopalian friend smiles at the audience and offers them the greatest hope any pastor ever promised a congregation: "But more importantly than your touching God . . . God can touch you."

DO NOT EXPECT THE SAME EXPERIENCE YOU HAD TWO
OR TWENTY YEARS AGO. YOU WILL HAVE A FRESH EXPERI-
ENCE, AND GOD WILL DEAL WITH YOU IN HIS OWN WAY.
—DWIGHT L. MOODY

QUESTIONS AND CONTACT

You may reach the author through e-mail at
www.elmertowns.com.

Best-Sellers
from Regal

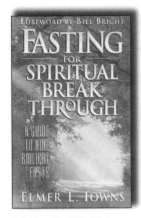
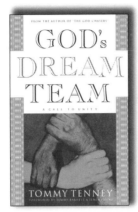
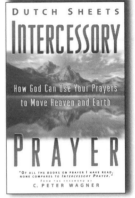
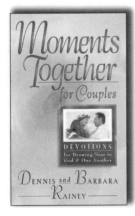
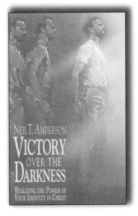
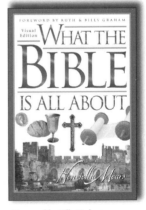

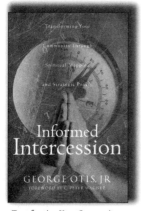

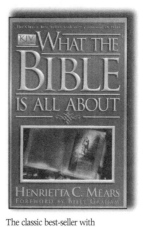